T0159102

OUR
COMPASSIONATE
KOSMOS

AWAKENING TO THE PRESENCE
OF CELESTIAL LOVE

Ricardo Horacio
Stocker Ph.D.

BALBOA
PRESS
A DIVISION OF HAY HOUSE

Balboa Press books may be ordered through booksellers or by contacting:

Balboa Press
A Division of Hay House
1663 Liberty Drive
Bloomington, IN 47403
www.balboapress.com
1 (877) 407-4847

Print information available on the last page.

ISBN: 978-1-5043-4563-7 (sc)
ISBN: 978-1-5043-4564-4 (e)

Balboa Press rev. date: 08/16/2019

DEDICATION

To our children:
Franziska Laura
Orion Cristiano
Morgan Ignacio
Santiago Alexis
And their children:
Jakob Benjamin
Otto Celestino
Mia Sophia
Anella June
Ricardo William
Polly S. Clementine
Mary Deborah
To the Bright & Beautiful Mothers:
Deborah Elizabeth
Faith Lucille
Amy Rianna
Hadley O'Neill
To loved-ones& friends
To my Mother & Father
To Pope Francis, the Dalai Lama, and
To all Peace Workers!

ON THE TITLE

Why Kosmos with K? Because the original Greek word pointed to the infinite Order and Harmony of the universe, different from cosmos referring to outer space. Other authors, (Whitman, Wilber) also use Kosmos. And the true meaning of "Compassionate" refers to a profound empathy and love,(not pity) for the condition of ALL beings!

CONTENTS

PRAISES

"What a delightful book! In these times of global dismay it is refreshing and uplifting to read such a book as 'Our Compassionate Kosmos'. Ricardo Stocker gives us a positive vision of the world, one that emphasizes Diversity, Purpose and Love. Dr. Stocker has found 'hidden splendor' in the universe, and shares it in a friendly manner that is articulate, poetic and inspiring."

Stanley Krippner Ph.D., Professor of Psychology,
Saybrook University, co-author of "Personal Mythology"

"The moment I encountered 'Our Compassionate Kosmos', the book emitted a vibration that entranced me. I am thankful to the universe and destiny for allowing me to come across this book. Reading it was as if time & space had opened a bubble for me to experience it. I can only hope that it will have the same effect on others. I think that it will open the minds and hearts of many, once they are exposed to such wisdom and love"

Abigail Au, College student

"In the midst of the chaos and misery across the planet, this timely book reminded me of a different road for Humanity to take. It is a joy to read these words, brought together clearly with such love. Thank you Ricardo for inspiring me, opening my mind and warming my heart at this critical time!"

Christopher Frederick, TV Documentary movie producer, UK

"When I first read the opening chapters of your book, a statement just burst out of me: 'I have finally found my place in the universe, in Life!' Your book brings so many things together for me. I find it hugely comforting, taking my soul and thoughts to wondrous places. I wish all your readers good blessings, for where their minds and spirits will go in reading this book"

Daphne Macneil, Neuro-education Specialist

INTRODUCTION

In the process of journaling for more than thirty years I discovered, and keep discovering, how every single day is a wide open door to what I call the "Newniverse." Indeed, every day and moment creates an actual possibility of receiving "fresh *life* from the Infinite;" new tides of awe, wonder and miracles, and a totally new, unprecedented opportunity to unfold gifts and potentials. Something utterly *new* can be received, and also given from the depths of Soul and Self.

When the decision came to select, gather and compile entries from my many journals into a book, I became excited and inspired with the idea. But soon I realized the difficulty of deciding what to include in the manuscript. Literally thousands of meditations, contemplations and mini-essays to choose from!

Another challenge has been, and continues to be, the choice of style, as I am also a poet, and when trying to articulate states of consciousness I can easily blend prose and poetry. And the result is that some of my essays can be considered prose-poems, and some of my poems mini-essays! I have introduced some of my poems throughout the book to express insights and intuitions differently.

A third, ongoing, challenge is the choice of particular words in the attempt to capture meanings and express ideas. Words from Metaphysics, Science, Poetry, Religion and every day usage are woven into a tapestry or symphony, hopefully "transparent to transcendence." This is why I have included a glossary of terms, and expressions of other authors and poets. At the end I added a list of "Inspiring Souls, Sources, and Resources," as references for those interested in further spiritual explorations.

So, here is it, a collection of meditations, contemplations and essays gleaned and gathered from my personal and mystical adventure of unfolding and evolving in an awesome Newniverse!

Villa Platonica 2017

HOW TO READ THIS BOOK

You can read it in a linear fashion, or you can do it in a non-linear way, opening it up anywhere. There are jewels hidden in the chapters. It may take more than one reading to find them. Enjoy!

FOREWORD
BY STANLEY KRIPPNER PhD

A ll of us need an internal roadmap to help us navigate through the life we have been given. Various names have been used to describe these roadmaps – personal mythologies, life schemas, belief systems, and many more. Whether we are aware of them or not, they impact the decisions we make and the roads we travel. For some people, there is little choice; each day presents a struggle to find food, shelter, and safety. For others, navigation is difficult because there are conflicting sets of directions. Our genes may steer us one way, but our family might push us another way. Our own motives and aspirations may be trumped by religious, ethnic, or cultural rules and regulations. Whether we are aware of this tug-of-war or not, personal choice may be confounded by the time and place that immerses our every waking moment.

Ricardo Stocker's book, *Our Compassionate Kosmos*, is a valuable resource for those of us who are aware of our struggle to construct a road map in these times of global miasma. Through his skillful use of prose and poetry, he shares what he has learned from his own life experience as well as from the wisdom of noted philosophers, historians, mystics, cosmologists, and artists. Indeed, Ricardo has prepared a moveable feast and has invited us to the banquet.

For Dr. Ricardo, there is no difference between the sacred and the profane, the natural and the supernatural. Nothing is static or written in stone. Instead, there is an endless flow of possibilities, as each of us wend our way on our evolutionary journeys. As we find our way through life, we are often joined by kindred spirits who are eager to share this adventure. Moments of re-awakening may shift our direction at any time. During these precious moments we may realize that the heart is as crucial as the mind, that external service and inner solitude can supplement each other.

To his credit, Ricardo does not avoid facing the "dark forces" that may throw us off track, nullifying or thwarting our valiant efforts. A comprehensive road map needs to acknowledge this darkness and provide resources that put us back on the road of light and love. For Ricardo, everything in the universe has at least a spark of light and love and he shows us how to let every breath we take keep that spark alive and vibrant. The spark can be fanned by our intuition as well as logic, by risk-taking as well as common sense. The spark can be nurtured by silence, mediation, contemplation, and relaxation – times when the Compassionate Kosmos is more readily realized. At these times, what is difficult to put into words often can emerge in art, music, and ritual. These expressions need not be linear; Ricardo sees the pitfalls of harboring the notion of "progress" as a superordinate goal. Rather than focusing on horizontal progression, Ricardo reminds us that depth & height often can yield greater riches.

For Ricardo, "true love" is free from exclusivity and possessiveness. There are many forms of true love, ranging from helping a neighbor to the adoration of Nature in all its variety. Ricardo provides "homework assignments" to assist us to anchor what we have learned. But when all is said and done, Ricardo's vision of Celestial Love remains a shimmering beacon. His wondrous book can help us draw our own road map, one that will keep us on track, holding high our banner in the great parade that unifies rather than separates, joins instead of divides, and flows seamlessly throughout what is rightfully called "the great chain of being."

Stanley Krippner, Ph.D.
Alan Watts Professor of Psychology, Saybrook University.

HUBBLE MAKES ME WOBBLE

In my youth, under the southern skies,
in the remote expanses of Patagonia,
I contemplated the sparkling heavens.
The Southern Cross, the Magellan Nebulae
and the innumerable stars of the night
I pointed my binoculars here and there
more and more worlds everywhere!
And my heart trembled at this vastness.
Today, Galileo's dream became Hubble,
the wonder telescope beyond the atmosphere.
And through its crystal eyes picture by picture
the unfathomable Kosmos unveils its glory
My mind wobbles at this immensity!
Is it possible? There is actually no end to it,
And no end means no beginning – boundlessness
Infinity and Eternity, here and now, and we in it!
Universes appearing and disappearing
as we breathe, countless worlds
and myriad souls unfolding, thriving,
evolving, blossoming and merging back
into an ocean of Celestial Light.
We have invented clocks, calendars
and calculators
to measure the unmeasurable
to explain the mysterious.
But, what if Alpha and Omega
are at this very moment happening?
What if all this glory is actually
our own story?
What if there is no time, but the timeless Splendor
between heartbeats?

CHAPTER 1

A TIMELESS UNIVERSE

OUR INFINITE HOME

How big is the universe? The answer to this question has been changing dramatically in the last 500 years. Since Galileo's telescope, and all the developments of modern astronomy, up to radio telescopes and the Hubble Space-Telescope, the vision of the Kosmos has increased and exploded exponentially. As a youth in Argentina, I remember stepping out into the sparkling winter night in our family's ranch in Patagonia. Reclining on an easy chair, and holding a pretty large navy binoculars, I would scan the heavens contemplating the Southern Cross, the Magellan Nebulae, and myriad stars and clusters. Once I had a wireless radio with me, tuned it to a classical station. I remember contemplating the fathomless vastness of the universe at the sound of J.S. Bach's flute and harpsichord sonatas. I was filled with awe and wonder. Was this the "Music of the Spheres?"

At other times the never-ending immensity of the universe brought very different feelings; feelings of meaninglessness, existential angst, absurdity, alienation, etc., recalling Pascal's words: "The silence of cosmic space terrifies me." The picture of a dead, mechanical, random, totally unconscious Kosmos, developed by 20th century science, had contaminated my soul! Now I know better, and the beautiful, amazing pictures revealed by the Hubble telescope bring back the "music of creation." But most importantly, they show more and more the incredible vastness of the Kosmos, to the point that we are beginning to wonder: "What if the universe literally has no end?" "Could this also mean that it has no beginning either?" (Both in time and space). Three implicit conclusions arise of these awesome possibilities. First, if the universe is truly infinite and timeless (eternal), then it is ever "beginning" and "ending," moment to moment. Second, our concept of "evolution" as it applied to life on earth, is expanded to zillion evolutions going on simultaneously, across infinite space. Life and consciousness are no longer confined to this tiny planet, but they are exuberantly unfolding in myriad worlds.

This also means that there are incredibly high, advanced and evolved Beings and "civilizations" across the ocean of galaxies. Furthermore, Earth and Humanity are not unfolding/evolving in isolation (like a freak cosmic phenomenon), but in profound interdependence (and harmonic resonance) with innumerable higher Kingdoms. Infinite Consciousness, or as R.W. Emerson called it: "Immense Intelligence" is not a "result" or "product" of cosmic evolution, but its very source and matrix.

And thirdly, each human soul, as an individualization of the macrocosmos, is also evolving and unfolding in infinity and eternity. That is, no one is confined between conception and death, but comes and goes from and into "other worlds," weaving lives and existences across all manner of celestial bodies (planets, stars, etc.). This also implies that our true "biography" is as beginningless and endless as the Kosmos itself. Furthermore, creation/evolution is not just happening to us, we are actually doing it!

To be alive is to *be* Life. To be conscious and awake is to *be* Light. To actually care for other beings is to *be* Love! Reversing the assumptions of materialistic/reductionist science, we can say that the whole Kosmos is alive, conscious, and loving. For mystics and visionaries across the ages this was, and is, an experiential fact, an obvious, basic, fundamental Truth.

NO BEGINNINGS

All across the Earth, peoples of all times and regions have wondered about the origins of everything in the universe, and where the Kosmos itself comes from. Accordingly, we are now aware of hundreds, if not thousands, of creation stories around the world. Myths, legends, philosophies, religions, ancient and modern cosmologies all share the vital need of making sense of cosmic existence – nature, life, humanity, the universe... For the last hundred years or so, we have now the "official" story, that is, scientific theories about how everything came to be. And as Joseph Campbell pointed out, other peoples' religions are for us "mythologies," but our religion is *not* a myth but a doctrine, a belief in *the* truth. Similarly, current scientific theories are not considered "stories," but descriptions of factual events. The prevalent cosmological view today is the so-called "Big-Bang Theory," and it is considered the "official" account of cosmic origins. But this theoretical map is being challenged and seriously questioned from various quarters, both from within and from without scientific domains.

A growing number of physicists, mathematicians, cosmologists, and other scientists are sobering up to the profound reality that this immensely vast, complex, diverse, exuberant and beautiful universe not only did not explode into existence (ex-nihilo), but also did not "begin" at all! The concept of time itself is being challenged. The very proposition of "no-beginnings" also implies that we as souls are timeless.

From without science the "official" theory is being challenged by the mystics: those who are intuitive and sensitive enough to experience first-hand the vast realms of consciousness. There is also a fast-growing community of thinkers, poets, metaphysicists and artists who, through a direct realization of the "Ground luminosity" of Being have reawaken to a highly spiritual and conscious universe. Shamans and Lamas, Yogis and Roshis, Poets and Philosophers, Mahatmas and Initiates, Mystics and Saints, all across history, and today, confirm again and again the reality of a sacred Kosmos!

At this point one may ask: Why does it matter in people's personal lives what theory or cosmology is the scientifically accepted? It matters because it permeates textbooks and the media, it influences education with a very one-sided picture of "reality," and it creates the impression that science has a monopoly on the "Truth." But psychologically, it matters the most, because there is a profound relationship between how we think about the universe and how we think and feel about our lives on Earth. Also, there seems to be a "cognitive dissonance" between "official science" and religious faith, which tends to generate a split in youthful minds. The good news is that a fascinating process is underway. True, leading edge scientists – fresh and open to the great mystery – are already proposing a worldview that, when widely recognized, would make many textbooks obsolete!

In various scientific fields, such as physics, medicine and psychology, for instance, the role of consciousness as a cosmic phenomenon is being increasingly researched. Intelligence, in a universal sense, is not confined to brains. It is an organizing cosmic force that manifests on different levels throughout all kingdoms. Returning to the question: How does the general, official, and scientifically "accepted" current worldview affect the individual's sense of meaning? If the universe, and all things and beings in it happened to be products of mere chance, haphazard, as Bertrand Russell put it: "the accidental collocation of atoms," then each life or biography becomes a random event, a meaningless act, in a mechanical, blind, and even hostile Kosmos. But thanks to the insights of sensitive, leading-edge 20th century philosophers, poets, artists, and scientists, the reductionist and atomistic worldview has been seriously questioned, and in many ways transcended. And the view and vision of the outer and inner universe seems to be changing so fast that some textbooks are lagging decades behind.

As a college professor I receive several free copies of textbooks, mostly in the field of Psychology, Communication, and Social Sciences, and related journals. The subject of "Consciousness," for instance, tends to be relegated to "altered states," pathology, neurology, sleep and dreams, and in a few notable exceptions to evolutionary levels of intelligence and the possibility of higher realms of knowledge. One can still detect a basically materialistic assumption that permeates textbooks. Then comes quantum mechanics, non-linear dynamics, chaos theory, and other breakthroughs that totally turn the old paradigms upside down, but they are too "advanced" or "far out" to be introduced to youthful minds. So they have to plough through mountains of mostly obsolete "facts," theories, and maps of "reality" that hardly correspond with the territory. So, to feed their visionary or mystic hunger the youth would turn to phantasy and fiction, to spirituality and metaphysics, to eroticism and mysticism. And of course, to mind-bending booze, drugs, music, video games, or extreme activities. Anything that would get them "out of their heads!" I always wondered if there is a correlation between curriculum (what they "have" to study) and adolescent behavior. The intuitive level becomes "allergic" to abstract information unrelated to true cosmic reality – that we are actual souls, deeply rooted in the universal oversoul, and already existing in an infinite sea of consciousness!

A most basic human need is to be in touch with "what is really going on." In our heart of hearts we already know it, but through the mind, or intellect we learn to articulate and formulate it. When reason and intuition are in harmony, we grow and thrive in consciousness. Otherwise there is a split and a struggle; a conflict and a friction; dissociation and dissonance, and inner and outer confrontation. My origins and my purpose are one. So are my alpha and my omega, where I come from and where I am going. The Source and destination of my being are also one. So is my existence as an individual, life on earth, and the whole universe all aspects of my true identity.

"Gnōthi seauton" -- "Know yourself" – was the Ancient Greek dictum – "Know yourself and you shall know the gods and the whole universe!" The more we recover our own soul wisdom and remember our true cosmic identity, the more clear we become about what we are not – the reductionistic, quantitative delusions of "official knowledge." The dawn of mystical common sense supernaturally dispels all obsolete, abstract nonsense!

Recently I heard a radio interview with a university professor on Economy. He said something fascinating: "The official textbooks on various aspects of Economy are becoming increasingly obsolete, as the present national and international situation challenges theoretical models about how the economy is supposed to work." I took this to be a clue and a symptom that the "maps" no longer correspond with the dynamics of the shifting "territory." And this is also the case with many fields beyond Economics. Indeed, the world in its many aspects and domains, is changing faster than "maps" can be drawn or textbooks written! How to keep up with this ongoing change and momentous transformations? Beyond the acceleration of information exchange and the flow of "intelligence" through the cybersphere, there is a way. This is the way of the awakening heart, the illumination of consciousness, which instantly puts each soul truly in touch with that is really going on! This is mostly a "vertical" attunement with Heaven and Earth; with Life and the Universe; with the ceaseless unfoldments of infinity and eternity as they happen! But this mystical alignment and timeless awareness is not at all "otherworldly," in fact, it is truly practical and "down to earth." This "vertical" awakening translates into a most creative, efficient, and effective "horizontal" awareness and action.

True activism and evolutionary change is rooted and centered in this subtle and sublime attunement with the heights and depths of Kosmic Existence. Advanced metaphysicians and physicians; mystics and scientists; artists and sensitive souls, all come together in the field of "no beginnings and no endings," the common goal of Realization. There is only One infinite Moment and it is the timeless now, or (as the title of Jean Gebser's book) "The Ever-Present Origin." Creation and Evolution is not a "long ago" event, it is actually happening, full force, this very moment! And I should add, it is happening in, through, and as each one of us right now!

> "Consciousness is infinite, unbounded and eternal, which means it has no beginning, it has no end, and it has no edges or boundaries in time."
>
> Deepak Chopra

FOUR WINDOWS TO THE UNIVERSE

How do I know what is really going on? There are basically four sources of "news." Two are "horizontal" and two "vertical." The most external, superficial and common is the main media, daily reporting events and all manner of happenings, some significant and many trivial. As we know, this is a huge filter controlled by corporations. The second source is what's called "alternative media," public radio and television, books, magazines, articles and investigative reports that attempt to illuminate what's beneath the "official news," what is covert, hidden, "secret," or "under the table." The main intent here is "increasing transparency."

The third source is less and less "horizontal" and more and more "vertical," as it derives from the experience of individuals who seem to have broken through the surface of average consciousness into higher and deeper realms of knowledge and Wisdom. This experiential source comes from the lives and Realizations of "Great Souls" (Mahatmas), Initiates, Saints, Heroes, Masters of Beauty, Truth and Goodness. From their works, Teachings and Presence, cosmic "news" and fresh tidings about "what is really going on;" regarding the true nature of Reality, can reach us. This source includes the "revelations" of Mystics and Geniuses. Here I would like to mention that every year the Watkins Bookstore Magazine (published by the oldest Esoteric/Spiritual Bookstore in London) puts up a list of "The hundred most spiritually influential living people." Not only writers, but a wide spectrum of souls, articulating and embodying the New Consciousness. And their lives and works are literally influencing millions across the world.

Though this third source provides a tremendous opening and access to vast realms of consciousness, it still remains as external information or "second hand" experience, for those not yet fully awakened to sacred-cosmic Reality.

The fourth source (which in truth is actually primary) is the direct, experiential, existential, "first hand" Self-Realization of our own Individuality. The awakened, illuminated Heart truly knows, instantly "what is really going on," both within and without, in the Soul and the universal Over-soul. It is through this blossoming into Cosmic consciousness; this "vertical" re-awakening or re-attuning of the soul to its Celestial Home-Source, that all the Wisdom of the third Source makes real sense. Before the awakening of the Mystic Heart all the spiritual information of the third source remains as "second hand hearsay." But as soon as the Soul re-members it-self, the timeless Wisdom of the Ages makes perfect, clear and obvious Sense!

And I say "re-awakening" and "re-membering" because the quintessential spirit within our Heart of hearts, always, already, as ever shines as a sacred star. And it becomes hidden and covered by thick layers of oblivion and denial in the process of embodiment and descent into gravity, density and "civilization." Re-membering and reawakening is ever-aflame at the sacred core of the soul.

When this illumination happens, one of the stunning Realizations is that of a profound re-cognition that we already knew this Light very well! As if recovering from a traumatic amnesia, we suddenly re-member our true identity, not only through time, but through space and eternity as well! Thus, we can instantly realize "what is really going on," not just in this contracted here and now, but in the infinite context of ceaseless (and beginningless) Kosmic Creation and perennial Evolution across the galaxies.

All across the spectrum of "needs," from the most basic survival, to the most transcendental, there runs the fundamental necessity to be in touch with "what is really going on." From biological, socio-cultural and spiritual sources this "knowledge" is provided. In early childhood mostly through sensations, feelings and intuitions. Then, increasingly through thinking and external information, Education, and Media. These are "horizontal," first and second sources mentioned above. The Spiritual or Soul-Quest begins to draw from the third source, from the reports of the "awakened ones." But, all along, the "Intelligence of the Heart" is ever-alive and waiting, like a buried seed, to break through, sprout and bloom in the Celestial Light of Remembrance!

MYSTERIUM TREMENDUM

The *Astronomy* magazine, in a recent article called "A Brief Appreciation of Galaxies," states that so far astronomers now estimate the number of galaxies to be around 125 billion! This makes the number of stars unimaginable large. And, of course, these estimates are based on what our current instruments are able to detect. So, chances are that there are still a lot more galaxies and "island universes" than our mind can fathom.

This cosmic immensity, this unfathomable ocean of galaxies seems to be literally boundless, infinite! But not only in size and vastness of space, also in complexity, exuberance, variety and diversity. What this means is that above and beyond all known or identified "Kingdoms," levels or realms, such as minerals, plant, animal and human, there is an immense spectrum of realms, domains, dimensions and levels of beings and consciousness across the universe. There is nothing new with this concept. It has been referred to as "The Great Chain of Being;" the Terrestrial and Celestial Hierarchies; or The Ladder of Kingdoms, etc.

The implication here is that what we understand as "Energy," Matter, Life and Human Consciousness, is a very small bandwidth of an immense spectrum, or a "color" of a vast "rainbow" of Kosmic Reality. Ascending the ladder of realms we notice that there are very few basic energies: gravity, electromagnetism, strong and weak forces, etc. Then we have discovered the "table of elements," one hundred or so. Further into the kingdoms of life, plant and animal, everything explodes into an amazing variety and diversity of species, types and kinds, from microorganisms to mammals.

As we consider the Human Kingdom per se, each particular, unique individual is a manifestation of a greater diversity, from DNA to destiny. Humanity, at the level of self-consciousness, already presents a pretty complex variety of specimens and souls. But moving higher into the Hierarchy of Kosmic-conscious. Beings, the diversity again explodes into an unimaginable variety. Above the Mahatmas, Saints, Great Initiates, Paramhansas, there are Avatars, innumerable and diverse as the stars, and yet all reflecting facets of the One! Furthermore, the realm of the Angelic Hierarchies presents an unconceivable variety and diversity, from Guardian Angels to Archangels, all the way to the Cherubim and Seraphim. Trillions and zillion gods and goddesses across the galaxies! So, we have three Infinites: Infinite Space, Infinite "time," and an Infinite Diversity of Beings.

INNUMERABLE EVOLUTIONS

One of the greatest discoveries or revelations of contemporary science is the unimaginable immensity of the Universe; its stunning endlessness and beginninglessness. There seems to be no point of darkness in the Kosmos. Wherever appears dark, focus a powerful enough telescope and innumerable stars and galaxies appear! Even the so-called "black holes" seem to be neither "black" nor "holes." Theories and descriptions abound. An astounding corollary of this realization (that "Infinity" is not just a mental abstraction or construct, but our actual existential "Home") is that evolution, as we understand it so far (stellar, geological, biological, cultural and spiritual), is happening simultaneously everywhere across the Kosmos.

What this means, in terms of consciousness, is that there are, at this very moment, countless planets or worlds unfolding or manifesting the whole spectrum of consciousness, from simple to self-consciousness, to Kosmic Consciousness and beyond. This implies the existence of very advanced civilizations and evolved Beings all across the galaxies. Advanced far beyond what we call "technology," and evolved in significantly different "bodies."

Another implication is that these "Elder Brothers and Sisters" take care, or take "under their wings" those planets or beings in earlier developmental stages, just as adults look after children. So, not only myriad cosmic civilizations coexist within

15

an immense rainbow of consciousness, but there is a profound intercommunication going on. It may be that our concept of "communication" tends to be very limited and confined to a kind of linear rationality. There is also a telepathic, soul to soul, heart to heart communication happening. When it is a profound connection between beings we call it "communion."

The existence of other worlds and higher Beings seems to be the common ground of all religions on Earth. We are just beginning to wake up and realize the cosmic meaning of Diversity as an incredible, awesome and glorious variety, plurality and multiplicity of worlds, domains, dimensions, Kingdoms and Beings!

WE SHALL ALL RECALL

Every single soul
struggling through all manner
of darkness, density or gravity;
through worlds, realms and domains,
Shall step by step awake to the Light.
Through lives, deaths and trans-formations,
Sooner or later each Heart re-members!
Whatever the journey, the drama or the story,
each one shall realize the glory;
The Kingdom, Power and Perfection;
the Infinity of Love, Goodness and Beauty
suffusing all cosmic existence.
As the solar splendor floods the Earth,
so each unique sentient being
is ever-blessed with sacred life, light and love!
It is all here already,
within, without, throughout,
animating, permeating, energizing
all souls, lives, and destinies.
So we shall all recall the whole
that is the essence of each Soul!

CHAPTER 2

CONSCIOUSNESS AND KOSMOS

KEY THOUGHTS ON ILLUMINATION

Here are some key thoughts regarding Illumination; Enlightenment; Cosmic Consciousness and Awakening:

1. This next stage or level of evolving consciousness is exuberantly more diverse than the common, generic, average level of "normal self-consciousness"
2. Already now embodied on Earth, there are individuals, at least a few millions, that have crossed the threshold into Kosmic Consciousness, or the Conscious Noosphere. (See Appendix I)
3. It is becoming increasingly easy to awaken into Illumined or Mystical Consciousness, as the whole "morphogenetic field" is energized both from Above and from Below, that is, from the supramental Intelligences, and from awakening humans reinforcing the field.
4. Because of number 3, also the planetary elements and the cosmic rays, energies, and particles reaching Earth, are increasingly charged with Higher Life, Light and Love, with Divine Prana.
5. The counterpart of the contamination and despoiling of our planet is the infusion of Celestial Nature into the Earthly spheres. Supernatural, Celestial, Miraculous energies and emanations are literally "in the air," in the

Light of the Sun, in the waters... The whole planet is being irradiated and suffused by heavenly beams.

6. In the process of this cosmic awakening, millions of human bodies are becoming increasingly able to feel, heal, capture, and assimilate these subtle substances and refined cosmic forces.

7. The perennial truths of Before and After Life, Reincarnation, Karma, Psychic-sacred Energy, the Power of Spirit over mind, over body; and the presence of tremendous possibilities for change, healing, transformation and Evolution, are increasingly Realized.

8. Illumination is not an "altered" state of consciousness, bizarre or abnormal, but a super-natural extension of every-day awareness. In fact, it is pure, "unaltered" consciousness.

9. It is an all-inclusive state. Sleep, dreams, trance, normal and paranormal, supernatural and divine, all infused and embraced by Infinite Light

10. It cannot be forced, "induced," taken by effort, fight or struggle (though there is a widespread illusion that it can be "broken into" through will-power). Surrendering to the grace of space, that is omnipresent, allows the Celestial Influx!

11. It is not something remote, alien, unreachable, but the very nature of our Beingness, the actual quintessence of who we already *are*.

12. It is "an-amnesis" (Plato), the opposite of forgetfulness or divine oblivion. It is remembering our stellar soul or celestial nature, and at the same time being fully embodied "down to earth."

CELESTIAL WINDS

The atmosphere surrounding our planet is not only a combination of elements, gases, particles, etc., but it is suffused by exuberant cosmic rays and by the subtle emanations of countless beings, both terrestrial and celestial. In other words, it is saturated by rainbows of consciousness. Today, the "air" is significantly different from decades and centuries ago, not only in terms of chemistry (including increasing Carbon Dioxide), but most importantly alchemically and psychically. An increasing spiritual luminosity and diaphaneity is now irradiating the whole atmosphere. This aspect of what is "in the air" has been called the Noosphere (See Appendix I) – the vibrant, living and luminous layer of Higher Consciousness.

As the "air" is also saturated with electromagnetic frequencies – the cybersphere and all manner of telecommunications, so it is psychically and spiritually charged with the thoughts, feelings, and intentions of billions of souls, from the densest and darkest to the most luminous and delightful. But the great difference with other times in history is that today the Power and the Presence of Great Souls (Mahatmas) and their correspondent degrees of cosmic consciousness is such as to neutralize and transmute darkness or "evil". We are truly living in "Pentecostal" times. The Holy Spirit is indeed "in the air," totally accessible to open and daring Hearts!

Indeed, "The answer my friend is blowing in the wind!" (Bob Dylan) "A fine wind is blowing the new Direction of Time" (D.H. Lawrence). And this "Wind" is the Spirit of the Times, the Celestial Power of St. Michael and his angels confronting and transmuting the Dragon of materialism, consumerism, ignorance and denial of the sacred in the universe. The Great Archangels of Cosmic Awakening, leading hosts of Luminous Angels, and in Harmony with Avatars, Boddhisattvas, Mahatmas, Great Initiates and Saints, are charging and recharging the atmosphere with Cosmic-Celestial Prana. This Higher Prana, vibrant with Hierotrons (sacred "particles") Divine Love and Infinite Intelligence, that is, the highest emanations/vibrations imaginable, is now in the very air we breathe. To assimilate its blessings, gifts, and graces, an uplifted, luminous Imagination is needed.

We may think this is just "make believe," or pretending "as if," a wishful, "magical" thinking, but the "mystical fact" is that the Cosmic-Sacred; the Divine; Heaven itself, is truly omnipresent, that is, already here permeating, saturating and animating all souls and worlds. Hence, we are already breathing the Kingdom, the Power, and the Glory. Let us reawake to this fundamental Reality!

> *"One of the very best exercises you can do is to imagine*
> *that you are breathing-in Kosmic Light, that intangible,*
> *quintessential Light that permeates all Creation. Let this Light*
> *penetrate and circulate deep within you. And as you breathe-*
> *out project it outwards to illuminate and help all beings"*

Omraam Mikhael Aivanhov

A BIG SURPRISE

Saints, Mystics, Mahatmas, those who had a near-death experience, and many illuminated souls, return from lofty, subtle, sublime and divine realms with a common message: "We are all in for a Big Surprise!" A surprise is an encounter with the unexpected something out of the ordinary—extraordinary. In this case, this "Big Surprise" involves a total reversal of consciousness ("conversion") in which all "rational" or common-sense interpretations and expectations about "reality" dissolve and melt in the Radiance of Reality. On the whole, this tends to be a three-fold shock.

1. One aspect of it concerns the Realization that Life and Death are one, that there is no such duality: that everything we thought of as dead is truly alive, from beings to the whole Kosmos. We assume that everything and everyone is in the process of dying, that is, aging, running down, decay and entropy. But then comes the revelation that there is a tremendous Power of integration, synthesis, growth, and perpetual rebirth at work/play throughout the universe. A glorious Creation/Evolution *is* in progress now! And this all-permeating, animating, Infinite Life is joy, fun, Energy, "Eternal Delight," Bliss, Ananda.

2. Another aspect of this Big, Shocking Surprise is the realization that the Light of Consciousness, which is

Intelligence, saturates and irradiates all realms and Kingdoms. Even the hardest metals and the darkest, densest worlds and souls are touched by the Light of the Logos. No one is truly "unredeemable." No such thing as "unconsciousness!"

3. The third facet of this shocking revelation is about Love. It reveals itself as the Sacred Fire within all beings and things. It is Warmth, Care, Tenderness, Kindness, Peace, Harmony, Beauty, Agape-Divine Love for "all sentient beings." And even down to the "frozen fires" of hell, Love is there. We had assumed that what we consider "evil" is such due to a total absence of love, and the great surprise is the revelation that Love is truly and totally omnipresent, an infinite Presence at the Heart of Reality, at the radiant core of all micro and macrocosmoses.

In summary, this Big, Shocking Surprise of the Mystical or trans-dimensional Revelation consists in the overwhelming realization that:

All is alive, all is *life* beyond "life and death."
All is conscious, all is *light* beyond "light and darkness."
All is good, all is *love* beyond "good and evil."

The very Radiance of our sun (who is a Beam of the Infinite, vibrant, Living and most loving Logos), is the quintessence of Life, Consciousness, and Love. As we learn to relax and surrender to its sacred warmth, and allow outer and inner splendors to merge in the One Beloved, so do we remember ourselves as Holy Flames of the Infinite Fire-Agni. Blessed be this omnipresence of Perfection!

TRANSFORMATIONS OF CONSCIOUSNESS THROUGH HISTORY

A s we survey the cultural developments and transformations along the whole history of humankind, we cannot fail to notice that the way we perceive and experience the universe has undergone several changes throughout different historical periods. Each period resonated a particular mode of consciousness, a cosmology or understanding of the world. To clarify these transformations of awareness, we could divide, very roughly, the whole evolution and history of consciousness in four distinct modes.

a) The Pre-historic or Ab-original Mode
b) The Ancient Mode
c) The Modern Mode
d) The Contemporary Mode (also called "Post-Modern")

Certainly, these modes or qualities of perception interpenetrate and overlap, so we cannot fix beginnings and endings of precise dates. Also, it is important to keep in mind that today, though we are immersed in the fourth mode, the other three are also present and active, not just as memory but as actual experience. That is to say that the Pre-historic mode never actually "ended"; it went "underground." The same with Ancient and Modern modes. It is all comprehended in the collective or archetypal unconscious in which all experience is transmuted into impulse, all past into future within the Eternal-Now.

How do these modes relate to the history of science? On the one hand these stages and levels of awareness are the very biography of science, the process of knowing reality and tuning in to its rhythms and cycles. On the other hand these ways of perceiving the universe show that science as such only emerged as distinct from religion and art during the transition from the Ancient mode to the Modern mode; that is, during what today we call the Middle Ages.

What are the special characteristics of these modes?

A very useful tool to help us understand these very different ways of relating to the Kosmos is the concept of the "*gunas*." Ancient Indian thought differentiated three basic modes of existence and called them: *Sattva, Rajas,* and *Tamas.* Each *guna* points to a particular cosmic dimension, and this triad itself denotes a hierarchy of realms, that is a "sacred order" of being or existence within the vastness of worlds.

Sattva is the realm or modality of Being, Luminosity, Intelligence, Cosmic Mind, Clarity, Divine Transparency, Spirit.

Rajas is the realm of Energy, Activity, Dynamism, Power, Force, Movement, Vibration and Waves.

Tamas is the aspect we discern as inert matter, substance, elements, particles, weight and gravity.

So at the highest level we speak of the celestial radiance of Beings (*Sattva*) emanating subtle and highly refined energies and substances. These energies descend, de-grade, or in-volve manifesting as forces (*Rajas*) and the whole spectrum of vibrations. These forces and waves condense further, manifesting in turn as elements, substances and the inertia of "solid matter" (*Tamas*). This is the darkest, heaviest, denser and coarser realm.

So, if we apply the triadic concept of the *gunas* to the understanding of the modes and their inter-relationships along History, we are able to develop new and fresh insights into the nature of each mode, and into the whole process of consciousness transformation throughout the ages.

a) The Pre-historic or Ab-original Mode extends far into the remote evolutionary past. Its main aspect is the discovery of the celestial nature of fire and its mastery for earthly purposes. The first-hand realization that all fire comes from the sun and that both are sacred manifestations of divine beings. All of Nature, the whole universe, is experienced as permeated, suffused and woven through with an exuberant multiplicity of Beings – Celestial Beings, Nature Beings, Elemental Beings, Ancestors, Animal Spirits, etc. Nothing can exist without spirit. The very "form" of things shows the presence of "spirit." Every "thing," even apparently lifeless objects, has a "soul." Modern and contemporary minds have looked back, or rather down, on this Ab-original consciousness and tried to explain it away with labels such as: animism, spiritualism, or archaic mysticism, pantheism, nature worship, etc.

The pre-historical, ab-original or primeval mode of consciousness, seems permeated with a *Sattvic* predominance, that is consciousness or awareness illuminated by the presence of countless Beings. Everything that happens is a direct outcome, or emanation of Beings. There is no such thing as chance or "accident." The "destiny" of every single creature or being is woven by the vast cosmic intelligence of myriad Beings. What today we call Mythology was developed at a later age and contains remnants and clues to the insights of this Ab-original mode of experiencing universal existence. There was no difference between sacred and profane, supernatural and natural, the "other" worlds and "this" world.

b) The Ancient Mode of consciousness emerges as a new way of perceiving the multiplicity of realms and the regularity of events. It is the birth of mathematics and the quest for the Logos, the laws and intelligence behind events. There is a noticeable shift from *Sattva* to *Rajas*, that is from the dimension of Being-ness to the realm of forces and powers. The gods, goddesses and plenty of spiritual Beings are still there, but this new emerging awareness begins to differentiate the forces and energies from the Beings themselves.

A new sense of separation and duality sets in. The dream-like awareness of "other" worlds begins to recede into the background and a "down to earth" focus begins to unfold. This manifests into magnificent architecture, sculpture, art and recorded language. Memory begins to be "objectified" in glyphs. Ancient Science is founded on the principle of cosmic correspondences. The dictum "As above so below" is the key that sounds through the ancient mode of consciousness. A sense of polarities and opposites permeates this newly awakened faculty of discrimination. Now there is a distinction between the "sacred" and the "profane," between the "inner" temple and the "outer" side (pro-fanum). Also a clear boundary is drawn between life and death, "this" world and the "other" world. The awareness of *Sattva* is somehow removed from "earth" and placed in "heaven." The emphasis is now on *Rajas* as the interweaving of forces and energies harmonizing the celestial and the terrestrial spheres. We see a struggle towards equilibrium; sometimes manifesting in static, rigid forms, sometimes appearing in dynamic, flexible ways.

For thousands of years, across many civilizations, Science unfolds, first as a quest for "vertical" correspondences, and then becomes more and more "horizontally" oriented. This increasing emphasis towards understand the workings of "this" world and applying this knowledge to improve survival and consolidate power over the "unruly," "unclear," "obscure," "mysterious" aspects of nature, lead to a progressive alienation of Science from the sacred, from *Sattva*, from Being-ness, from Religion.

c) The Modern Mode of consciousness starts manifesting with increasing clarity after the first millennium A.D. Though the ancient gods and goddesses have somehow disappeared into other realms, still there is a feeling for the "celestial intelligences" weaving through the Kosmos. But something has changed radically, the Light, the Fire, that hitherto was brought down by the deities, now has become available "within." Gautama became the Buddha not by borrowing or receiving, but by Self-kindling the innermost Light. The Christos demonstrates and announces, "The kingdom of Heaven is within you!" So, that ocean of intelligence in which all worlds interpenetrate and have their Being, is now rapidly reduced to a drop of "reason" within a human skull. During the Renaissance transition to the modern mode, a new set of correspondences is discovered–this time between "within" and "without" the microcosm and the macrocosm, the individual and the universe. A new center is found: The Human-Being, Humanism. Also the Sun, a self-illuminated Being, becomes the center of the world. The key-note of Modern consciousness is sounded in the words of Shakespeare, "I can be bounded in a nutshell, and be the King of Infinite Space." Out of this new awareness infinitesimal calculus is born.

And through incredible measurements and calculations man eventually descends on the moon knowing exactly what his weight will be. In a period of a handful of centuries we witness a tremendous increase and diversification of knowledge. A multiplicity of sciences expanding into all realms, penetrating the innermost workings of all kingdoms. The emphasis has now moved from *Rajas* to *Tamas*. The focus is now the elements, substances, "matter," the main tool, a deepening "analysis." We still speak of forces, energies, vibrations, but with no reference whatsoever to "Beings." Suddenly the whole universe appears as a vast and complex "machine." Books on "celestial mechanics" are written. The cosmologies of Newton and Descartes prevail and permeate the scientific world. Then, as Darwin, Marx and Freud enter the stage, we are left with a predominantly *Tamasic* world view, all is reduced to matter, chance, blind forces, numbers, pieces.

The industrialization of the world, and the tremendous technical achievements in all fields are all fruits of this Modern mode of consciousness, which find it's culmination at the middle of the twentieth century.

d) The Contemporary Mode of Consciousness begins to emerge with tremendous momentum at the birth of the twentieth century. Through the arts, sciences, social movements, wars, and fresh spiritual impulses, something totally new on a planetary scale begins to stir within the hearts and minds of millions. The darkest and densest hours, the loss of "solid reality" starts to break down under the melting radiance of a cosmic fire released upon the earth. Not only powerful stellar energies blast away solid matter, but the very concept of material reality is transmuted. Matter is now seen for what it is: an illusion, both conceptual and perceptual. Frozen clots of energy in the mind-freezer. The leading edge of the contemporary mode of consciousness is re-cognizing and re-discovering in a new light, the realm of *Rajas*. Universal reality is seen again as an ocean of energies and deeply interacting fields of force at all levels. Though at the vanguard of Contemporary consciousness, the breakthrough has already happened, the tremendous inertia of the Modern mode still permeates today's cultures with obsolete or anachronistic mind patterns.

In all cultural and scientific fields, we begin to see clear trends toward transcending modern reductionism and towards a symphonic integration of disciplines.

When we take a close look at what is actually happening in the realms of New Physics, New Biology, Psychology, Ecology and many other sciences, we quickly realize that the flow, quality of perceptions and information shared is opening up a multi-dimensional vision of reality that strikes an harmonic resonance with the Ancient mode of consciousness.

An alchemical marriage of Science and Spirituality is happening. Artificial boundaries belonging to out-dated mind-sets are naturally melting away by a new kind of planetary mysticism. This, for example, is what we see in Deep Ecology, the rebirth of Shamanism and the growing trend towards spiritual growth and awakening.

Where we used to only see "organisms" or "animals," now we begin to perceive Beings.

This awakening towards the Being-ness of all species, all races, all individuals is resonating with deeper levels of the archetypal unconscious, with the Ab-original mode of consciousness. This awareness goes beyond the "natural" world, it includes the world of the so-called "dead" and higher realms of super-natural or cosmic Beings.

In other words, the blossoming of Contemporary consciousness comprehends and re-integrates the other modes in a process of on-going transformation and spiritual evolution.

The graph on page 36 shows the relationship of the three *gunas* to the four modes of consciousness and its changes in time:

Many philosophers, such as Hegel, Bucke, Steiner, Gebser, Wilber, and a great number of thinkers and sages, have attempted in their own way to describe the transformations of Consciousness through history. There are plenty of evolutionary and historical "maps" depicting ages and stages; eras and epochs; seasons and modes of human consciousness all along Humanity's development. But there is an underlying, simple and fundamental theme: The past was radically different from the present type and kind of consciousness. And so will the future be significantly different from the present, but with a deeper affinity with the remote past, yet transformed and transmuted afresh.

Using the concept of the "Gunas," from Hinduism, I attempted to describe and point to the subtle, yet significant differences in worldviews across the ages. The curve in page 36 diagram shows a descent and an ascent (also an archetypal theme). We could say that the bottom of the curve points to the last ten to twelve centuries, when the increasing "progress" of civilization systemically obliterated ancestral and cosmic memories. It is also possible to say that the twentieth century was the darkest hour of "fallen" human consciousness; the time of most intense forgetfulness of our cosmic/celestial nature. Yet through the '60s, the '80s, and the beginnings of the third Millennium, many hopeful signs indicate that we are now in the ascending curve towards the re-discovery of Being. The first significant sign was the scientific realization that "matter" as a solid reality does not really exist. Underlying it is the now famous "Quantum Field."

It seems that it is all pure energy in flux. And the spectrum of energies appears to be far more complex, diverse and vaster than it was thought to be. The second crucial sign is the increasing realization that Consciousness itself is a cosmic phenomenon not dependent, or generated by brains; that it exists across many worlds and is not obliterated by the death of the body. This arises through the testimony of many Mystical and Near-Death Experiences. A third, and most significant sign is the increasing availability of spiritual traditions, practices, and teachers through the cybersphere.

There are many other indications, such as Marian apparitions, crop circles and literally millions and millions of people praying and meditating daily, that point to a fresh awakening of consciousness all over the Earth. We *are* crossing the threshold into a new era of planetary-wide spiritual/cosmic awakening!

"There are superior forms of Intelligent Life in the Universe which are making contact with us by various means. We may enlarge our capacity to solve all our problems by giving recognition to , and by co-operating with, this Higher Wisdom which is being made available to us."

Anthony Brooke

The Universe Experienced as an Interaction of:

		Ab-original	Ancient	Modern	Contemporary	Future
Spirit Religion Wisdom	Sattva					Beings and their Emanations
Heart Intuition Artistic Imagination	Rajas					Energies Forces Waves
Reason Intellectual Abstraction	Tamas					Things Objects Particles

A KOSMIC FIELD OF BLOOMING MIRACLES

I n this glorious, unfathomable, infinite, ever-unfolding, evolving and continuously trans-forming universe, nothing and no one is fixed, static, permanent, or constant. Out of our three-dimensional, rational, abstract consciousness we have conjured up a fixed, frozen concept of cosmic reality.

Concepts such as "matter," "iron laws," "written in stone," "status-quo," "universal constants," "monumental," "monolithic," etc. all denote a solid, unchangeable conception of the world. But the actual truth (discovered by the Ancient Sages, mystics of all times, and leading-edge scientists of today) is that there seems to be a perpetual, dynamic flux of ceaseless trans-formation at all levels of reality.

Things, conditions, situations and people, may appear to be continuous, "the same," permanent, or static, but at deeper or higher levels there is an ongoing flow of trans-formation and transmutation. Indeed, there is an infinite, dynamic Field of tremendous probabilities and immense possibilities ever-boiling and bubbling up with exuberant manifestations.

In this vast, unmeasurable, celestial ocean of consciousness, beings and things are perpetually coming into form, and out of form; "materializing" and "de-materializing;" embodying and dis-embodying. Indeed, we are all actual miracles of Existence! So is the whole Kosmos a Field of blooming miracles!

THE OTHER "MISSING LINK"

In the "Great Chain of Being," human beings stand between animals and other higher Kingdoms. Humankind was considered above the realm of the beasts and "a little lower than the angels." The Theory of Evolution got rid of the possibility of any "Kingdom" above the human, and relegated human beings to the category of primates. Hence, Paleontology became focused on the possibility of finding intermediate stages linking hominids to modern humans or "*Homo-sapiens-sapiens.*" This double "sapiens" refers to the human characteristic of self-consciousness, to the fact that humans seem to be aware that they are aware.

Contemporary researchers of consciousness tend to argue about the relationship between brain and mind. There is a whole spectrum of theories, from the hard-core materialistic view that brain = mind, to the "quantum consciousness" idea that Mind = Cosmos.

The "transpersonal," spiritual noetic interpretation is that the whole universe is permeated, saturated, and animated by Consciousness, and that the human brain/body translates and transmits aspects of consciousness uniquely.

Space *is* "Mind at Large," and all manner of organisms "tune in" to different bandwidths of a vast spectrum, an immense "rainbow" of possibilities, just as the diverse sensory capabilities of animals.

When it comes to psychic, paranormal, ESP, or metanormal, extra-ordinary or "miraculous" phenomenon, there are two general attitudes: a) they are impossible, b) they are possible through the existence of subtle energetic Fields (vibrations, frequencies, etc.).

Here is where the other "missing link" comes into play. This is the re-discovery and realization that there are several realms or "Kingdoms" above the human, including angels, gods, avatars, extraterrestrials, and a great diversity of Kosmic or Celestial Beings of a different evolutionary order.

For Mystics of all times and places this is obvious. Saints, Initiates, Shamans, Mahatmas, Sages and Paramhansas the world over, not only declare the existence of many natural and supernatural spirits/beings permeating the universe – all Kingdoms, but also assert that a profound interaction and communication is ever at work and play.

Here is the foundation of Prayer, Meditation and Contemplation, as a profound attunement with the domains of Kosmic Beingness.

"There are many things between Heaven and Earth, Horatio, that you have not dreamed of in your philosophy!" (*Shakespeare*). And I should add, "in your official science!"

Lorna Byrne, a contemporary Irish Mystic, who seems to see and communicate with Angels and Archangels, has written several international bestsellers. Thousands line up for hours at her book signings, and to get her blessings. Why this appeal? Where is this worldwide interest coming from? I believe that this is a symptom of a collective re-awakening to "The Great Chain of Being;" that a rapidly increasing number of souls are re-membering and Realizing that Higher Kingdoms not only exist, but that a sublime communication is indeed going on!

AN IMMENSE EVOLUTIONARY JOURNEY

"Each one of us decides to incarnate upon this planet
at particular points in time and space. We have
chosen (under celestial guidance) to come here to learn
a particular lesson ('to bear the Beams of Love')
that will advance us on our spiritual evolutionary
pathway." – Louise Hay

Our evolutionary journey is immense, vast, literally infinite, and encompassing innumerable embodiments throughout countless worlds. Each one unique, particular, special, yet woven in perfect Karmic/ Dharmic harmony with everyone else, with all beings. In the boundless freedom of divine space there is choice, the actual possibility of deciding which way to go. The belief in chance, haphazard, luck or fate is a poor excuse. Yes, there are mistakes, errors, misses (the true meaning of "sin") falls and blunders, but it is all part of the original learning, the continuous evolutionary adventure. All levels of teachers, mentors, instructors, and masters take us "under their wings" as trainers and coaches, ever nurturing, guiding, encouraging and inspiring us to actualize and manifest our unique treasure of potentials, gifts, and graces. And we do the same for other unfolding souls. So we are always learning and always teaching, ever receiving and ever sharing and giving; continuously gathering and distributing. Nothing and no one is static, fixed, unchangeable. There is a glorious, cosmic Flux; a ceaseless transformation, a continuous, dynamic process of evolutionary metamorphosis and transfiguration.

As growing, thriving, unfolding Beings we are, exist and evolve within the vast hierarchies of Kingdoms. So, at any particular stage we belong, partake, and share with various Kingdoms and levels of beings. There are Celestial and Terrestrial (or planetary) hierarchies, also called Universal Brother/Sisterhoods, to which we belong, knowingly or unknowingly, consciously or unconsciously. We join in attunement with these "Rainbows of Being" in accordance with our own "colors" (vibrations/ emotions), in various degrees of Luminosity or dullness (opacity or darkness). There exists, within each Heart, a center of sacred choice that allows us to decide where we want to belong, who we want to associate with or emulate. Beyond "class," profession, vocation, or lifestyle there are those "kindred spirits" and soul mates with whom we come together to share aspects of the immense quest!

"Birds of a feather flock (and migrate) together!"

OUR GREAT ADVENTURE

We admire and enjoy great adventures. We read about them or watch plays or movies in which souls go through all manner of experiences and challenges. There seems to be a profound vicarious delight in the contemplation of others' trials, quests, struggles, and adventures. But what about our own "great adventure"? We may think that our daily, mundane, lives do not quite qualify as an "adventure," as they lack excitement, novelty, fun or discovery. But this feeling of "ennui," meaninglessness, boredom, daily drag, "the same old" routine, "going through the motions" or lack of enthusiasm, arises out of the cloud of oblivion. We have just forgotten the immensity of the Big Picture; the Kosmic scope of our true adventure through innumerable worlds and embodiments.

As soon as the twilight of Remembrance begins (again) to break through the darkness of "amnesia," and we "come around" to our true identity, then dawns the realization that our journey/quest/adventure is as vast and unfathomable as the Universe itself. Then we are reminded that we too are deeply involved in an amazing, fantastic and tremendous Adventure! Others' stories just trigger aspects of our own unique journey across the stars. This is why legends, folk tales, myths, fairy tales, novels, movies, biographies and all kinds of stories are enticing, thrilling or inspiring. "We shall not cease from exploration" sings the poet T.S. Elliott, pointing to a ceaseless, Kosmic adventure. But so is our stellar background, vast, profound, and immense as Creation itself!

Being a human being on planet Earth is already an awesome adventure, considering that we are actors/participants in the Great Drama/Quest/Story of unfolding/evolving Consciousness. As Emerson remarked, "there is no such thing as History, only Biography." And this is the story of each Heart and Soul *across* aeons and worlds. Not only many lives, incarnations and embodiments, but also adventures through other worlds and realms in-between, and all across Systems and Galaxies! Thank God for forgetfulness, so we can focus on one life at a time, and as Thoreau said: "One world at a time!" But as we are ready to Remember, we can re-awaken to our true Infinite and Glorious Adventure!

Each soul, each unique Individuality, each human being is called to re-member and keep on with their own "true adventure." Not only do we forget our particular quest as we enter the oblivion of "civilization," but also we fall "under the influence" of traditions and others. Thus, we attempt to recover meaning through imitation, and through vicarious living. To exist and live vicariously means not to live your own life; your own particular adventure/quest, but to think and feel through others' experiences. The all-pervasive power of the Media, with its relentless tsunamis of information, makes it very easy today to get lost in "entertainment," and "watching" everybody else's lives! But sooner or later, hopefully before our last breath, Kosmic re-minders come our way to bring us back into our "true adventure," the quintessential purpose or "assignment" that brought us into this particular life in the first place.

We are always surrounded by all kinds of "Kosmic reminders," that come into our lives as situations, challenges, other people and inspirations from Celestial sources. The more attentive, alert, aware and sensitive to this continuous stream of clues, hints, indications and illuminations; the better the possibilities of recovering our true purpose, call, quest or adventure. First of all, we are not here to repeat, mimic or copy anybody else's destiny or dharma, but to bring forth; to birth; to express and manifest something utterly *new!*

There is something new, different, unique, fresh, unprecedented, and divinely special that is pressing from the Kosmic depths of each soul, to unfold and blossom in the light. On the surface, there may be lots of similarities with other lives, stories, styles or "biographies," but essentially, each one's evolutionary journey among the stars is unique and ever-new. The Universe, Heaven and Earth, countless souls and beings, innumerable Presences, are continuously "broadcasting" signals to our Heart of hearts, as "Kosmic reminders." All manner of "practices" are there to facilitate our "reception;" to truly listen to what is really going on in our own spiritual adventure; to fine-tune to our deepest and highest Dharma-quest, Great Adventure.

All around the Earth in all continents, landscapes, and countries, at any given moment, day or night there are souls, millions upon millions tuning-in, in harmony with Celestial Light. Innumerable men, women and children praying, meditating, contemplating and playing with Delight. Through them, (though small in numbers compared with billions) Divine Power is grounded. This is the true, transformative, evolutionary Power ceaselessly descending from Heaven to awaken us. All other man-made forces cannot resist or distort this all-penetrating Celestial Influx.

And as every day thousands of Hearts Light up and open-up to this ever-present glory, and more and more souls increasingly Re-member their stellar essence, and Great Adventure. So do profound, radical and significant changes occur. Indeed, we are rapidly coming to the end of History as we know it, time becomes space and in this Grace all inner and outer boundaries disappear. Every day now, the Universe is calling us by our secret names to step out of the trance and join the galaxies in their evolutionary dance!

INVITATION IN THE WIND

There is a vibrant spirit in the Wind,
there is Consciousness in the air, and a
new, fresh revelation in the Noosphere!
Indeed, "The times they are a-changing!"
Tremendous trans-formations underway
awakening Hearts and Souls across the planet
The "horizontal" news are troubling enough,
but the "vertical" tidings – what is Really going
on in Heaven and Earth – are fantastic, glorious, miraculous!
Subtle tsunamis of Celestial Love sweeping through
and uplifting souls into Kosmic Remembrance!
Suddenly, in the silence and stillness of meditation
the splendor of omnipresence reveals itself, and in
its Radiance appearances become transparent to
the glory *that-is*. Real Truth, Beauty and
Goodness manifest spontaneously as
Infinite Light, Divine Harmony, Order and Perfection.
In every-one, in every-body this blessed possibility
exists and waits… till the Spark recognizes the Flame,
till the soul hears its own celestial name!
We are all invited to this magnificent celebration,
to this alchemical Wedding/Evolutionary Initiation.
Please, R.S.V.P. now, don't delay, you are more
than welcomed; the Beloved is actually expecting *you*!

CHAPTER 3

THE PRESENCE OF CELESTIAL LOVE

UNIVERSAL LOVE

We are put on earth a little space, that we may learn
to bear the beams of Love. – William Blake

Though Love has been divided into many kinds, such as filial love, brotherly love, love for ancestors or descendants, passionate/romantic love, love of god, self-love, love of nature, etc., in its essence, Love is One, a Kosmic Energy that holds worlds and souls together.

Out of this central Flame of Mystical, Universal Love, innumerable rays shine in all directions, touching Hearts with a vast rainbow of possible loves. There is always the danger of one-sidedness, of obsession or fixation; of exclusivity.

A powerful one-sided, exclusive attraction can easily generate compulsion, obsession, fixation and madness. Compassion, a comprehensive empathy for the condition of all beings can counteract one-sided tendencies.

True Love, pure Love is totally unconditional and free from exclusivity and possessiveness. It is the Holy Fire of quintessential Beingness already, as ever, at the Radiant core of all hearts and souls across the Hierarchy of Kingdoms. The re-awakening of a single Sacred Heart has a tremendous influence on innumerable souls!

"Love is all you need," as the Beatles confirmed, and *you* is all that Love needs to share its Beauty and Glory further!

LOVING CHALLENGES

L ife, existence itself, presents to us a fluctuating series of challenges, difficulties, hurdles and all manner of "problems" to deal with. Whatever the presenting situation, there is always the vast, immense, kosmic background of Infinite Intelligence. And this underlying, overarching, all-permeating "background," is not just below, above, or behind our daily life, but suffusing every single moment and inch of our existential reality. Whitman called it "the Best of time and space." The Tibetans refer to it as the "Ground Luminosity;" and Christianity, as "the Light of the World," or the Living "Christos-Logos." Regardless of the tradition or terminology, this Omnipresence of timeless and Infinite Life, Light and Love is our true nature; the very substance and soul of our Beingness.

Thus, we are already, as ever, soaked through and irradiated with *It*, although we tend to remain unconscious or oblivious to *Its* vibrant Presence. Daily, survival demands, pressures and complications seem to be continuously pulling us out, sucking our attention and energies. But the instant we stop, become still, silent, calm and sufficiently relaxed, we allow this "background Radiance," "Ground Luminosity" or "Hidden Splendor," to shine through illuminating our awareness and consciousness of what is truly going on. And in this very emerging (ascending or descending) Light lie all solutions and resolutions to all kind of challenges (physical, emotional, mental, spiritual).

As a coach places hurdles to challenge the running athletes to jump higher, so are our angelic guides and "coaches" staging and orchestrating all manner of situations to encourage souls to attempt and dare "quantum leaps." For what purpose? To continue thriving; to activate our evolutionary potentials, to overcome "gravity" and "heaviness;" to beautifully rise to all "loving challenges" presented! Yes, "loving challenges," because behind, beyond and inherent in all existential challenges there is the omnipresence of immense, boundless Love! And in the ever-present Radiance of Kosmic Love, we are all, sooner or later, "macrowaved" into divinities! Thus, we are continually transformed and transfigured by the grace and most Loving "pressures" choreographed for the Highest Good for all concerned!

THE KOSMIC LOVE FORCE

The universal Force of Love; the Power of Celestial Love; the sacred/cosmic Energy of Love, is absolutely Real! More than that, it is the very foundation of Kosmic Existence! This Divine, ever-creative, nurturing, sustaining, healing, uplifting and illuminating Force or universal Power is omnipresent, all-permeating and animating. The main organ for its reception, transmission and expression is the Heart. Though the whole body, with all its functions and faculties, is an actual condensation and particular individualization of this Cosmic Energy of Love, the Heart Chakra, deeply linked to the soul, is most sensitive and open to the *Love Force*.

Scientists tend to associate and correlate Intelligence and overall consciousness with the brain. Obviously, there is a relationship there, but true Intelligence and Higher Consciousness are centered in the Heart, and transcend the "nervous system." There are many levels or dimensions of the Heart, such as the organic heart, the emotional heart, the intuitive heart, the compassionate heart, the Immaculate Heart and the Sacred Heart. The opening and blossoming of the Higher Heart allows the influx and circulation of the Kosmic Love Force; the Divine Power of Healing, Transformation and Evolution!

PRAYING = BEING

As the Heart and the Soul are in ceaseless communication; in a continuous spiritual and telepathic contact ever sharing tides of Earth and Heaven, and as the Soul shines in a state of perpetual prayer, ever in harmonic resonance with the Cosmic Oversoul, so is the Heart experienced in the Art of Prayer, as a soul's apprentice. The Heart knows how to pray, as the body knows how to move or be still and as the mind knows about Thoughts and Archetypes.

Deeply feeling the vibrant Presence in the Heart, is opening up to the ceaseless vibrations of Prayer ever-pulsating through our whole Being.

These luminous Soul vibrations/emanations are translated in the Heart as Celestial Love, Joy, Peace, Gratitude, Healing Compassion, Wisdom and Beauty. This is the core of Prayer at the Heart level. It is praise, play, adoration, celebration, "Eternal Delight"!

At the body level it is gesture, posture, movement, dance, ritual, sensations, pleasure, pain, life itself! And at the mind level prayer becomes words, images, statements, affirmations, petitions, contemplations, and all manner of articulations of the Word, the *logos*. To *feel* the universe in the Heart, to be *alive*, and to be *aware* and conscious is already to "pray without ceasing"! Prayer *is* "what is going on"!

ANSWERED PRAYERS

Whatever the thoughts or feelings that fill my inner life at any given moment, I know that they can be changed, trans-formed or transmuted by the Power of Prayer and Invocation. As soon as I invite and invoke the Presence of Celestial Entities, Angels, or the Holy Mother, they are instantaneously there, that is, *here*, as in truth they are always, already omnipresent!

It may seem that it is all a spinning of my imagination, a mere make-believe, but in my Heart I know better. And what I do know is that in body, mind, heart and spirit I am already divinely designed and equipped to communicate with Heaven; to syntonize with Higher Worlds and Beings; to be finely attuned to Celestial Souls and Kingdoms. Thus, to pray; to call; to invoke and summon the assistance, guidance, support or Light from the Sacred Kosmos, is a most natural, spontaneous attitude of the soul.

And this call, request, prayer or invocation can be general, or very precise and particular. It can be an overall soul-attitude of gratitude, joy, love, appreciation and recognition of the actual cornucopia of grace that is my life; or it can be a focused invocation regarding a particular area, aspect or relationship that calls for clarification. But, whatever it is that triggers my prayers, there is in me a profound knowingness that all the Light, all the Love, all the Life or Resources needed are already here, ever-available, omnipresent!

Whenever I experience tinges of melancholia, loneliness, neediness, or missing something or someone, I quickly remind myself that I can ask, call, invoke, pray and invite my Celestial Friends to Light-up my consciousness; to uplift my awareness, to re-awaken me to the glory permeating the Whole, Infinite Story! And the response is indeed instantaneous, totally beyond "time." "Ask, and it *is* given!" Not in a "future" sometime, but already, out of the Timeless Now. The question *is* the answer! Here is the deeper meaning of Self-inquiry. Who is asking whom? At first, it may seem that there is one soul invoking another, higher Soul for help or guidance. But the depths of prayer, meditation, or contemplation reveals that it is not a one-sided communication but a spiritual interaction and transaction, an actual Soul conversation or spiritual dialogue. And furthermore, it is the Infinite Oversoul ever-praying to It-self!

Here is the mystical meaning of Solitude and Silence! My prayers are always answered! How can that be? The very act, gesture, attitude or opening to welcome the ceaseless Kosmic Flow of Grace, is already accepting and receiving *it*! Heaven already knows what is "the very best for all concerned," so, as I align myself with the Intelligence of Higher Love; with the Light of the Oversoul, Perfect Guidance happens super-naturally.

THOUGHTS ON MARY

Avatars, those Celestial Beings that descend from "Above" embodying themselves as humans, not only incarnate as redeemers and transformers of consciousness, but also as Ideal Role Models pointing to the future of humanity. Their existence demonstrates the tremendous transmuting Power of the sacred; how the Kosmic/Divine Radiance of the Oversoul can totally transfigure, transubstantiate and trans-humanize what we normally call "the body." Out of celestial "particles," elements, energies and emanations a *new* body is generated; the Body of Glory, beyond time, gravity, "corruption" and death. The so-called "physical body" is to begin with a "scaffolding," mould or raw block out of which a Master-piece is created. It is a continuous transformative process that takes countless incarnations, but through the many chisel-strokes of experience the inherent Beauty of our quintessential divinity emerges as a Radiant Microkosmic Master-Piece. Officially, Mary's body "was taken to Heaven, body and soul." But in truth, She ascended super-naturally, "falling upwards," by Her own Levity, Grace and Celestial Power.

As an Avatar, Boddhisattva of Infinite Love and Compassion, Her Presence is an opening, a gate of grace between Heaven and Earth. Her many apparitions and miraculous manifestations across our planet are clear indications that She (with a whole constellation of Avatars) is most deeply, actively and lovingly involved with our spiritual Evolution, as humanity and as Individualities. As the Celestial Mother She is the Creative Power of the Oversoul, and is beyond all formalized Religion. Though She manifests her gifts and graces through all kinds of traditions, beliefs and "denominations," Her Stellar Being transcends all doctrines and dogmas. She is the fullness of Grace (*Gratia Plena*) and the very Divine Substance/Kosmic Womb of the Christ within (*Mater Dei*), the Mother of God right within each Heart and Soul. She and the Holy Spirit are One, Her Flame is one and the same! (In Hebrew the word for spirit –Ruach- is feminine) And this Holy Spirit of the Kosmic Mother is supreme, "supramental" Consciousness! All true Mystics and Mahatmas, Initiates and Paramhansas, Masters and Saints "breathe" directly into this "Anima Mundi (Soul of the World);" into the Holy Breath of the Mother! In the Radiance of Her Luminous Love we awaken!

There are many mysteries associated with Mary, for instance Her appearances under so many names, skin colors, & other features, that many have wondered: is she the same, one being? Other mystery is the reports of appearing at Mount Carmel on 850 B.C.! There is also her association with many other Celestial and Terrestrial Goddesses, such as Kuan-Ying, Isis, Tonantzin, Demeter, etc. She seems to assume multiple aspects of the Divine Femenine, and be an embodiment of Sacred Diversity Herself!

In the Summer of 2018 I visited Medjugorje and was amazed at the international devotion to Mary. Met people from all over the planet!

THE MYSTERY OF ONE-ANOTHER

As the mystery of the Soul opens up to the Heart and Mind, a Realization dawns spontaneously. This is the revelation that each soul, each-one (including myself) is in truth, many and simultaneously, that all possible souls are One. Each soul is a unique star, yet all stars partake in the One, Infinite Light of the Kosmic Oversoul. And I, as a Celestial Being, am not fixed, but journey across immensities, ever-dancing in circles and spirals throughout infinity. And as this Soul-Individuality, or sacred self reawakens to its own Background Splendor, it increasingly realizes or re-members its own unfathomable glory; its own beginninglessness and endlessness; its own Kosmic, divine nature. Its "Supreme Identity" with the Atman-Self, or the Universal Oversoul becomes clear and luminous, yet, this unique Individuality, or one-of-a-kind Expression of the Kosmic Spirit, remains intact as a unique, precious Flame, with a particular, self-chosen, Divine Purpose!

Thus, I celebrate and rejoice in this particular journey/Quest/ Adventure; in this profound involvement in Evolution; in this fantastic, celestial "assignment"! And I keep in mind, and in my Heart of hearts, the truth that each and every-one in the whole network/wheel of my relationships, is also a perpetually unfolding mystery. From my intimate loved-ones and friends, to all others coming in and out of my life, there is always an underlying Karmic/Dharmic link; a Kosmic connection of some kind that draws us together into all manner of "group projects," teams, troupes, communities, etc. As flocks of "migratory souls" we share seasons and journeys across the sparkling sea of galaxies, at times re-cognizing the unique Radiant Beauty of each Soul's "hidden Splendor"! Thus we are continually re-discovering the Glory within and through all possible stories including our own. And as we all share and partake of this "Ground Luminosity," no one awakens alone, because a Soul truly Re-membering it-Self, like a creative explosion of Luminous Love, touches, affects and shakes very many others into "coming around" and re-member *who* they really *are*!

All souls, all stars across this unfathomable universe are deeply related and interconnected at the "speed of Love," that is, instantaneously! And as each star in the Heavens belongs to innumerable constellations, according to the point of observation, the planet or the world, so does each precious, unique stellar soul relate to countless configurations, groups or communities of other souls. In this timeless/eternal net of suns, all partake of the One, Infinite Luminous Love! And through this omnipresent Celestial Love, they can be instantly in touch just by a thought, especially a loving or grateful thought.

Because of the complexity and profound Karmic and Dharmic interdependence through the immensity of reincarnations, any soul held lovingly in heart and mind is instantly contacted − regardless of countries, continents or any time-space conditions. Thus, I can as easily be in touch with Pythagoras, Debussy or my mother, through the mystical Love in my very Heart and Soul. And also, as souls are journeying, moving and passing from world to world, any-one coming into our lives or consciousness could very well be a "significant other" (Kosmically speaking). So, the web and network of all our soul-relationships, of all evolutionary significant loved-ones and friends, is in truth vast, immense, unfathomable as the Kosmos itself. Every-one we knew; every-one we now know, and every-single one that we shall get to know, belongs to our Kosmic Community, or immense, Universal Brother/Sisterhood. This is what Thich Nhat Hanh calls "Interbeing"

Love is the link, the glue, and the Power that is ever-bringing us together as flocks of transmigrating souls across universes and worlds! Indeed, "bird of a feather flock together," so do soulmates, kindred spirits and true friends across the infinite. But we are not stuck with one type and color of "feathers." On the contrary, our aura-wings are constantly changing, ever-reflecting trans-formations of consciousness. So, as we grow, evolve and unfold inherent kosmic/divine potentials, we can become different "birds." We can, for instance, move from chickenhood to swanhood, and eventually be transfigured into Great Swans – Paramahamsas. And in this ceaseless evolutionary journey come together with a great diversity of Kosmic Friends, celestial Loved ones, communities and constellations!

THE DESCENT OF CELESTIAL HELP

The study of helping behavior in animals has shown that there are natural tendencies to protect, care and support their own kind, and in many instances other kinds too. As distress signals are picked up so the instinct, tendency or impulse to help is activated. A dolphin in distress, for example, will elicit help and assistance from other dolphins. This helping tendency, of course, also permeates the Human Kingdom, but it also exists, with increasing clarity and intensity in all Higher Kingdoms in the vast cosmic Hierarchy or "chain of Being."

If we now consider the whole planet Earth as a Living, sentient and spiritual Being afloat, alive and conscious in the vast stellar sea of space, then we realize that it does not exist in isolation. There is a constant communication with Celestial Realms; a ceaseless exchange of signals, substances, energies and emanations going on.

Tremendous human activity in the last couple of centuries have obviously affected the ecological balance of the whole planet, from environmental degradation, destruction and contamination, to climate change. The Earth, as a planet-Being, is generating and broadcasting "distress signals" into cosmic depths. The universe is already aware of our plight, and help from innumerable stellar sources is actually streaming in. This celestial assistance is not new, it has been happening for millennia and even aeons, but at this crucial evolutionary moment it has intensified significantly.

I refer to this phenomenon as "the descent of Celestial Love." Many Mystics, philosophers, saints, Initiates, and Mahatmas have noticed and realized this actual heavenly downpour, and described it with terms such as: Grace, Influx, Divine Intervention, Apparitions, Descent of the Supermind, the Collective Superconscious, Visitations, Cosmic Contact, "Second Coming," etc.

Behind the many descriptions and interpretations there are basic premises such as the realization that our world is not a little ball floating in a vast inhospitable and indifferent Kosmos, but a Living Entity, an ensouled Being in perpetual communication and exchange with the Infinite. Another premise is that this cosmic interaction and exchange involves higher and vaster realms of consciousness. An "Immense Intelligence" is certainly at work and play! And beyond this is the sublime and "Most High" Power of Celestial Love, that is not remote but fully omnipresent, and totally, and instantly accessible by any-one!

And in the degree that individuals become instruments or embodiments of Celestial Love (The Power, the Kingdom and the Glory) they exert a tremendous, beneficial influence on World History and planetary evolution.

Avatars and Mahatmas (Great Souls) are living demonstrations of "grounding Heaven;" of manifesting Celestial Love "down to earth." The creative, harmonizing and healing Power of Celestial Love is the Highest Kosmic Energy/Emanation beyond our capacity to imagine, yet it is ever-Present, already aflame in all Hearts and stars!

THE REDEEMING POWER OF ADORATION

The Light and Delight of Adoration glows through the "rose-window" of my life. All aspects, domains, dimensions of my existence become illuminated from within revealing inherent gifts and graces. Daily actions and interactions with other souls are charged with the sacred Energy released by Adoration that discloses the core-divinity hidden in all beings, souls and worlds. To adore and to be adored is the recognition of this sacred-core, alive and aflame in each and all. Forms, bodies, beings, become translucent to the formless Splendor of the Over-Soul, within and behind every-one.

I believe it was Thomas Merton who said that if we could truly see and recognize this core-divinity, we would fall on our knees and worship one-another! Adoration opens the golden portals of the Heart to the Presence of Sacred Beingness across all Kingdoms, from rocks to gods; from stars to Avatars; from souls to souls; from atom to Atman!

All across the Earth, right at this very moment, literally millions of souls shine with the Holy Fire of Adoration, Love, Devotion, Prayer, Veneration and contemplation of the "Mysterium Tremendum." Not only in monasteries, ashrams, convents, temples and churches, but everywhere in cities and wilderness, towns, and country where Hearts and Souls are open grails to the Influx of Celestial, Luminous Love. This *is* transmuting inner and outer darkness!

SOUL BEAUTY

We are all striving for a higher Beauty; for a Beauty that is full of Light and Delight; for a Beauty that is Harmony, Peace, Wisdom and Compassion. Our culture is fixated on a beauty that is strictly confined to form, and can be cosmetically manipulated. But true Beauty manifests in a perfect, dynamic balance between form and formlessness. When the transcendent, the formless, is allowed to shine through the flexibility, plasticity, and versatility of forms, then divine Beauty glows spontaneously. The unborn, the unconditioned, the formlessness of pure space – which is grace, is omnipresent. A subtle, sacred, pressure from the depths of the soul is ever-ready to unfold its hidden harmony, joy and perfection.

Beauty's immense intelligence is super-naturally expressing it-Self through myriad forms, structures, organisms, bodies and Individualities. Forms can block, obliterate, or distort this expression. This is why trust, surrender, relaxation, silence, stillness, meditation and contemplation help to soften rigidities, and let the Splendor of Real Beauty through. The inherent Radiance and Kosmic Beauty in our Hearts and Souls and in the Oversoul is ever-manifesting in nature, in animals, in children, in Luminous Souls, in Saints and Initiates, in anyone, anywhere whose consciousness remains translucent to the Infinite. This is why in the process of recovering our primordial innocence, spontaneity, joy, wonder, playfulness and creativity, we allow the inherent Beauty of the Soul to shine through.

THE POWER OF CELESTIAL LOVE

What do I mean by "The Power of Celestial Love"? The great creative challenge of the *new* consciousness is to articulate itself into a clear, translucent common sense. This is also the universal challenge of all mystics across history: how to translate into language that which is beyond words; how to articulate higher and deeper levels or dimensions of consciousness. Initiates, Masters, Saints and Mahatmas across all cultures express their visions, revelations and realizations in most creative ways through philosophy and poetry, science and art, methods and rituals, stories and sounds, words and silence. I have chosen the words "Celestial Love" to describe something indescribable, yet by approximations, insights and glimpses can be articulated.

Using the symbology of the "gunas" from Hinduism, I could say that Celestial Love manifests in a threefold manner. At the densest and darkest level (Tamas) it is the fundamental Substance, the Mother-Matrix of all "elements" (Dark Matter?). Then it also manifests as pure Energy, Force and Power (Rajas). It is the ever-creative Energy of the universe, from Eros to Logos; the Evolutionary drive unfolding as Life and Light. And at its highest, divine dimension it manifests as Being (Sattva); as the Presence or omnipresence of Celestial, Kosmic Beings, Stellar Fountains of pure Divine Love − Bodhisattvas, Avatars, the Angelic Hierarchies, the Mother of the World.

The very Substance, Power and Presence of Celestial Love is already, as ever, right *here*, permeating, suffusing and animating all worlds, kingdoms and beings. Accordingly, it is in my flesh and bones ("This is my body"), in my very blood and all elements and "particles" of this body. It is the Life-Force, the "Elan Vital," the Living Pulse of creation/evolution in me, through me and as me. And it is the Presence of the Oversoul in my Heart; the Being I am, ever partaking of all Beingness.

Thus, I can truly declare: "I am an actual Individualization of Celestial Love." "In body, mind and spirit, I am a unique and precious condensation and manifestation of Infinite, Divine Love." And so is every single human being, every-one.

To re-member this and Realize it afresh is called "awakening." Awakening to what? To the tremendous and glorious omnipresence of Celestial Life, Light and Love, already irradiating all, and instantly experienceable through re-membering and waking up!

Immense, yet most gentle, tidal waves of Celestial Silence sweep through the galaxy. Our solar system and this blessed planet are touched and suffused by this Sacred Pulse that vibrates through all spheres and layers. All kingdoms and beings feel these cosmic swells streaming and moving in the depths of worlds and souls.

And this most Living and Loving Silence flows smoothly through all hearts and minds as Infinite Peace, Harmony, Beauty, and Perfection. It is a Presence, not an absence; a powerful pulsating omnipresence comprehending and transmuting all possible "noise," turbulence, chaos, influence, disorder or dissonance.

In this most natural and super-natural Silence of Heaven and Earth unfolds the wholeness and wholesomeness of each unique Stellar Self. The great Silence is here, right now happening, flowing, streaming, pulsating, moving as a vast cosmic current of Luminous Peace and Love, and all awakened Hearts partake of this swelling glory!

VERTICAL INFLUX

I f we only rely on the massive "horizontal" information provided by the Internet, the media, and all other "expert" sources, then, the global picture and the prospects for Earth and Humanity are indeed very bleak, hopeless and depressing. But, thank god, this is *not* the whole picture. There is another source of information, knowledge, wisdom, insight and revelation that illuminates the "Big Picture;" the "Immense Intelligence" of Divine Evolution at work. And this "vertical" information or syntonization (fine attunement with Heaven and Earth; with the Heights and Depths of Creation, Above and Below), reveals and discloses a universe brimming with glorious possibilities. Through this Mystical attunement many individualized centers of consciousness, or illuminated Hearts, provide openings to the ever-available Influx of supramental consciousness or Celestial Love. And through millions of "Enlightening rods," all over the planet, sacred-cosmic Energy is grounded, allowing Celestial Rays and Emanations to neutralize and transmute the forces and influences of "horizontal" darkness (the Michaelic Hosts *are* piercing, neutralizing and trans-forming the widespread Dragon of "Progress"!).

This blessed influx from innumerable stellar Souls and Sources downpours into the atmosphere charging the air and the winds with a glorious and Luminous Consciousness!

RE-AWAKENING

*"Enlightenment is the re-membering of the Buddha
Mind (already present in every sentient being) is
noticing that this simple, clear, ever-present awareness
is primordial purity just as it is" – Ken Wilber*

To live, function and operate on Earth we have forgotten Heaven. It is not a disgrace, neither a cosmic mistake, but a natural process of descent into this precious planet. We were prepared in advance, forewarned of the many possible consequences of oblivion. How we could get lost in the labyrinths of "down to Earth" rationality. How we could easily identify with flesh, bones, prestige and precious stones. How we could become entangled and trapped in gravity, density, solidity, materiality, and darkness. But we were also advised and most lovingly reminded that the holy possibility of remembering Heaven, the Divine Kosmos, our true Source-Home, The Big Picture, the Infinite Plan and the Purpose, *is* ever-present, alive and aflame in our Heart of hearts. We were also told that whatever happens, we are never alone. That we are always under the wings of the Angelic Intelligences, who instantly respond to our call and invocation. Divine Guidance and Providence ever available!

And finally, before incarnating, we were also told that this was not a random, meaningless adventure into Earth and Humankind, but an actual "assignment," a quest/adventure with a sublime purpose; a specific part in a grand play. All necessary "horizontal," survival learning may seem to intensify our forgetfulness of Heaven, but our Stellar Identity shall remain intact, pristine, immaculate. And true maturity, growth and spiritual evolution includes celestial re-membering. Yes, the very possibility of Awakening to our Ab-original Buddha Nature or Christ-Mind (Logos) is truly ever-present. At any moment, in a timeless instant, this Kosmic Re-membering we call Illumination, Enlightenment or Self-Realization, not only *can* happen, but sooner or later *will* happen! The existential challenge is "to bring Heaven down to Earth" as Aïvanhov put it. To awaken *in* the body allowing Higher Beauty, Truth and Goodness to further manifest on this blessed planet. To "vertically" re-member the Heights and Depths of our Being and to share talents and treasures with all sentient beings. We *are* "The Buddhas of Infinite *Light*," Eternal, timeless *Life*, and the Celestial, unfathomable *Love* of innumerable Mahatmas, Bodhisattvas and Avatars!

THE REALITY OF SACRED ENERGY

*"Keep your Heart on fire with a passion of compassion
for all beings, and keep filling (charging and
recharging) your body with Sacred Energy for whatever
work It calls you to do in the world."*
— *Andrew Harvey*

Here are the great re-discoveries and revelations that
fuel the Flame of the New Consciousness:

1. That the intelligence of the Heart far surpasses brain-bound "critical thinking."
2. That the Heart itself is a higher organ meant for the reception and transmission of Kosmic Love.
3. That Kosmic, Sacred Psychic Energy not only exists but is omnipresent, truly Powerful and miraculous.
4. That this sublime, Divine Energy is not just a "force" but an Emanation of Highly Conscious Beings.
5. That we are all, already divinely designed and equipped to "pick up," capture, assimilate, embody, or utilize this Sacred Energy for all manner of creative work in our world, and for the whole planet.

All across the ages Philosophers, Mystics, Poets and even
scientists discovered and realized that there is a vast spectrum of

energies weaving worlds. And this sacred Rainbow of multicolored Consciousness is reflected in myriad "minds" (subhuman, human and superhuman); from sentient beings to Mahatmas, Boddhisattvas, Avatars, Angels and the "Anima Mundi." And they, (as we are now realizing afresh) also discovered that the most sacred, sublime, subtle and divine Energies/Emanations are, already as ever, omnipresent, that is, fully Here and Now. Being totally Present, these Luminous colors of Higher Consciousness are also accessible, available, fully "at hand" (like the, or *as*, the Kingdom of Heaven) and "usable."

The Ancient Hindu traditions developed the idea of a spectrum of "Pranas" accessible through "yogas." But all sacred traditions referred to these Energies under different names such as: Light, Fire, Breath, "Supersubstantial Bread," Manna, Holy Spirit, Grace, etc. Consciously, Imaginatively and deliberately we can open up, relax, receive, assimilate and embody this Sacred Rainbow of Heavenly Energies and Emanations. As we do we spontaneously become "*the change*," *the trans-formation!*

ENTHUSIASM

Enthusiasm, excitement, great expectations and anticipations of wonderful encounters, events or things to come, is an uplifting and energizing human emotion. When we look forward, plan, organize, prepare or make arrangements for something delightful, fun, beautiful or loving to happen, all of our energies, forces, and capacities become focused, concentrated and united in a future goal or ideal situation. This is how we generate positive "Self-fulfilling prophecies," luminous expectations that mobilize and integrate our inner resources.

But the key question is about what kind of ideas or things trigger this enthusiasm. And here is where there is a whole range, a vast spectrum of levels or domains. What do we get enthusiastic about? Is it about getting some kind of satisfaction, pleasure or fun? Is it about money, sex, promotion, influence or some kind of power? Is it related to acquiring, owning, possessing or having something or someone? Is it about external, superficial, mundane, material things? Or is it directed to inner unfoldment, growth, transformation and spiritual evolution?

We all have things, events, or situations that we get excited about. Things that we would love to manifest, demonstrate, embody or realize. A fundamental question is about the actual source of our enthusiasm. Where is it coming from? Is it a mere reflection of superficial or "horizontal" conditionings? Or is it something related to the depths and heights of our existence? Is the propelling Force – the magnetism – coming from the past or from the Future? The very nature of our goals and ideals have a tremendous influence on our motivation and enthusiasm. What is moving us; what is mobilizing our inner resources, activating our potentials?

As there is a strong tendency "to become what we contemplate," as Plato remarked, so, the highest, more sublime and divine our Ideal, Role Model, Vision or Inspiration, the more propelling Energy (Evolutionary "rocket fuel") and true Enthusiasm we shall have. The Fire of Enthusiasm – the god within (En-Theos) – is the cosmic Power that brought us here, into this particular incarnation/assignment, and the more in tune with this ab-original Purpose, the more able we become to manifest our gifts, talents and graces as blessings to each and all; as benedictions for the world!

"Nothing great has ever being achieved without enthusiasm"

Ralph W. Emerson

SACRED STATISTICS

Every single day
as the planet turns in its dance,
About 360,000 babies are born on Earth.
And around 160,000 human beings expire.
Every single hour, there are around
10,000 births and 4,000 deaths.
At each breath we take, first breaths and last breaths
are happening all over this precious planet.
But there is another sacred statistic
that we don't hear about.
It is the fact that every single day, hour, moment
thousands of souls are waking up to the Light,
and breaking through into higher dimensions of consciousness
Aware of these ever-fresh, awakening winds,
I breathe-in, and I am inspired
by the countless Hearts blossoming everywhere.
I join the awakening waves of wonder;
the Winds of Celestial Grace!

CHAPTER 4

AGELESS WISDOM

COMMON THEMES OF THE NEW ERA

"To know the universe itself as a road, as many roads for traveling souls – all that was or is apparent upon this globe or any globe (moves apart) before the procession of souls along the grand roads of the universe." – Walt Whitman

L ooking into the lives and works of the great Souls, Mahatmas, Paramhamsas, Avatars, Initiates, Saints (East and West) of the last couple of centuries, I am struck by amazing common themes.

1. One central or key thought and Realization among the multitude of Mahatmas is that at the radiant core of our Being we are, already, as ever, divine; that our true Self or Identity is by nature Celestial; and that our earthly lives, or incarnations, are but tiny arcs of an immense (vast as the universe itself) evolutionary curve/spiral weaving/ dancing through innumerable worlds!

2. Another key thought concerns what is called: Karma-Dharma, which implies an Infinite Intelligence ever at work/play, orchestrating and choreographing all destinies, lives, existences... This, of course, is the opposite of old fashioned scientism (already becoming rapidly obsolete) that attempts to explain everything in terms of chaos,

randomness, haphazard, mere chance, and is also extremely reductionistic.

3. A third common trend that I detect refers to the methods, systems, exercises, disciplines, strategies, Sadhanas, yogas, paths or practices presented by Mahatmas in the last 150 years or so. Overall there seems to be a fourfold categorization of approaches: body-centered (somatic), Heart-centered (Devotion); Mind-centered (Metaphysics), and will-centered (service and social action). This explains the incredible variety of methods or "ways" available in the spiritual market today.

4. A fourth emerging theme or trend is the decreasing need for an external guru or teacher, and the emphasis on finding or making contact with the "inner guru"; the Higher Self, Atman within, the Kingdom of Heaven at the Heart's core. This ties up with the prophesy of Joachim de Fioris (13th century) that pointed to the third millennium as inspired by the Holy Spirit within each. This means direct and instantaneous access to the divine without the need of intermediaries or intercessors.

5. Another, and related, wide spread phenomenon has been referred to as "the thinning of the veil," or increased transparency between worlds. Between the natural and supernatural, the sensible and the supersensible; the mental and the supramental aspects of consciousness. Communication between worlds and souls is a lot easier than in the past. Straining and struggling are no longer needed to make contact to syntonize with spiritual realms. The global cyber-net is a crude metaphor of this increasing transparency, but it has a down-side or shadow aspect. The mental and psychic "noise" of this information explosion is tremendous. The "horizontal," centrifugal forces of distraction, confusion and "message overload"

are unprecedented. Celestial "reception" *is* stronger, but so is the mesmerizing force of the media.

6. As access to Heaven or Cosmic Consciousness seems to be increasingly easy or effortless (as predicted by Richard Bucke), and as the Celestial Energies/Emanations are downpouring Light and Love on the planet, so are the influences of Hell driven by the inertia, heaviness, and momentum of history, actively infringing on the human soul. The Media, sophisticated weapons, greed, hate, fundamentalism, fanaticism, destruction and distraction and all manner of influences stimulating the lowest and the worst of human nature are also present.

7. The good news, also announced by the Mahatmas, is that the Energies and Powers of Light, of higher consciousness and of Celestial Beings, are tremendously more powerful than the dark forces. Divine Luminous Love, the Sacred Radiance of the Spirit is truly omnipotent. It is literally All-Mighty, able to instantly neutralize, nullify or transmute any manifestation of "evil." This is why the Community of Mahatmas, universal Sister/Brotherhood, Hierarchy or "The Communion of Saints," by their mere Presence, in this and other worlds, not only counteracts and counter-balances the gravity of darkness, but most significantly is ceaselessly uplifting Humanity to Higher dimensions of consciousness and Being.

In summary, all these basic themes emphasized by modern and contemporary Great Souls point to, and converge in the Reality of a New Era. We have actually crossed the threshold into a New World, a fresh Age of Celestial consciousness! The inertia and mechanical momentum of the Past still exerts influence, but less and less. The Divine Power and Magnetism of the Omega, The Timeless Future, increases daily, summoning all Hearts to their quintessential Stellar Nature!

A NEW LANGUAGE

new Consciousness is definitely now coming into the world; into the whole planet. It is simultaneously descending and precipitating from sacred Celestial Heights, and emerging/arising from the Hearts and Souls of literally millions of individuals. This Influx and unfolding of a sublime and profound Kosmic Awareness presents many challenges, for instance, the confrontation of this Fresh Force of Awakening with the *old* inertia and momentum of historical forces and ways, rapidly becoming obsolete. The Old Testament ways of retribution, retaliation and revenge do not belong in the *new* consciousness. Neither the economic forces of perpetual growth and rampant consumerism, and all the environmental "collateral damage" that goes with them. Yet another challenge, that is subtle but significant, is the formulation and articulation of this *new* Light of consciousness into a living language that is both informative and trans-formative.

There is a profound relationship between consciousness and the way we feel, think, talk, write and communicate overall. One is always affecting the other. A new consciousness calls for a new language, a fresh articulation and a creative formulation of what we are becoming aware of. This is precisely what hundreds, if not thousands, of Spiritual Teachers, Artists, Poets, Scientists, Philosophers and Masters in numerous fields, are actually doing in their attempt to translate the new Light into Language; the *Logos* into the working Word; Consciousness into creative change.

This new, transformational language articulating the new consciousness illuminating the Noosphere, is a fresh, creative blend of many aspects and kinds of communication. And this new articulation of descending Light and blossoming Love, is now manifesting in a new, creative, integral, rhapsodic, symphonic, archetypal, Kosmic language. It is a fusion of Prose and Poetry, Science and Mysticism, Fact and Fiction, Cosmology and Psychology, Physics and Metaphysics, Reason and Revelation, Sound and Image, Verbal and Nonverbal, Silence and Light!

WAKING UP – WHO, WHEN, WHERE?

Scholars and students of the world's mystical traditions tend to emphasize the commonality or essential sameness across Religions; the central core of the creative experience or "supreme identity" with the Divine Cosmos. Words like Samadhi; Satori, Illumination, Self-Realization, Cosmic Consciousness, etc. are assumed to point to the very same experience of a break-through into the sacred, or transcendental nature of Reality. But many explorers into the depths, heights, and diversity of Consciousness present a different picture or interpretation. First of all, Consciousness, like everything in the Universe, is not static, fixed, or permanent, but in constant flux. As the weather, the seasons, and all manner of cosmic cycles, conditions and celestial configurations, consciousness itself is in a perpetual state of change, ceaseless trans-formation. Accordingly, the extases of Saint Theresa of Avila, the samadhis of Ramakrishna the psychedelic revelations of Ram Dass are *not* the same "spiritual awakening." Why? There are several reasons, but the main three ones are: they are three unique, different beings, with their own particular Karma and Dharma; their own evolutionary "biography" spawning ages and embodiments (reincarnations). The second reason is that whatever happened to them, it happened in a particular historic time (Spanish Renaissance, India – late 19th century, USA in the 1960s).

Both the historical times and the culture/civilization backgrounds were significantly different. And the third reason is that they were in diverse geographical areas. Not only Spain, India and USA represent different environments, but the very particular areas, regions, and localities where these experiences happened constitute a unique context that contributed to them happening. Another factor to be included is the developmental stage of each of these three sample-individuals. How old they were? How mature? What was going on in their lives? Etc. What all this means is that each unique individual in a particular time and place can experience higher levels and "colors" of consciousness according to their particular one-of-a-kind nature.

Comparing mystical experiences across the board (as many authors have done), and assuming a core-sameness, disregards the exuberant variety and diversity of these experiences, and their inner and outer contexts.

At any given moment, the entire inner and outer Kosmos (micro and macrocosmos) is teeming with awakening possibilities. As everything on Heaven and Earth is permeated, suffused and irradiated with Consciousness, even the very air we breathe (another meaning to "conscious breath!"), so we can say that spiritual awakening is in the air, as Love is, and Light, and Life! It is in the Atmosphere; in the Noosphere, in the "Atmansphere," in "the Infinite Celestial spheres!" Awakening happens, supernaturally! And in exuberantly diverse ways beyond imagination!

UPRIGHT AWARENESS

There seems to be a struggle between what appears to be going on according to the media, and what the depths of mystical meditation reveals. On a more personal level, this seeming struggle manifests as a tension between "horizontal" demands, daily "survival" and "maintenance" pressures and expectations, and the "vertical" mystery of attunement with the depths of Heaven and Earth; with the great, creative Silence of Being. The pullings and pushings of surface demands and information overload tends to generate stress and anxiety, an underlying, disturbing sensation of hopelessness, uneasiness, fear, and of being overwhelmed by chaotic events and forces. To counteract, neutralize and nullify these dark clouds and currents, the daily practice of meditation, prayer and contemplation enable us to re-connect with our "roots" and "wings;" with our true, transcendental nature; with our unique Holy Flame; with the Light of the Big Picture!

"Horizontally," the main tendency is to react; to react with irritation, anger, fear, anxiety or grief. Habits and "chain reactions" are deeply rooted in our upbringing, experience, background. It is all part of our shield, defensiveness, protection, "fencing" our own space. These reactions are automatic, unconscious, mechanical. Anyone or anything can "press our buttons" and it happens. This is the most common way of dealing with people or situations. The other, sane way, is the way of "vertical" self-awareness. This involves awareness of emotions as they arise; an inner space of detachment, and a non-reactive response. Being truly in touch with what is going on within; with the kind and quality of thoughts and feelings arising, moment to moment, in relation to others, events, places or conditions, generates the ability to respond. This is true response-ability, honesty, and uprightness. It requires flexibility, spaciousness, relaxation, trust and letting go of assumptions, expectations, rigid points of view and attempts to control and manipulate. There is always a Higher, vast, "Immense Intelligence" at work and play in all interactions and situations. It is the Kosmic Wisdom of the Heart, ever-available; the Infinite, universal Mind, ever-*new* and creative. And as we learn to rely and surrender to Its glorious grace, we allow the influx of fresh Life, Light, and Love to renew all areas and aspects of our life; to be Healed and Harmonized with the Infinite Perfection *that-is!*

HOW THE OLD TENDS TO CONTAMINATE THE NEW

All areas and domains of culture, such as Politics, Economics, Religion, Education, Art, Science, etc. have roots in History, in the past, both recent and remote. They are grounded and rooted in all manner of traditions. But, as the whole universe is in a continuous state of flux, change and transformation, so are civilizations and cultures under various pressures to change and adjust to the times, including the rhythms and cycles of nature and Kosmos. There seems to be an inbuilt resistance to change to let go of the "security" and comfort of established traditions. This fear of change generates rigidity, inflexibility, dogmatism, and fundamentalism (the root cause of practically most violence) in any given area or aspect of culture. It is as if the "authority" and shadow of the past continues to exert a powerful influence on the present, ever contaminating and clouding the actual newness that is unfolding.

Something totally new, fresh, and unprecedented is actually underway, happening now, day by day, moment to moment. But the tremendous momentum, inertia, and influence of the past keeps polluting the pristine perception of the ever-new. This happens collectively on a grand scale, and individually. The whole of History, and each single biography seem contaminated, or "infected" by the persistence of the "same old" patterns, mechanically repeating themselves. For instance, the old laws, both political and religious, seem to be "written in stone," that is, they are very difficult to change or transcend. From the Constitution to the Old Testament, there is a tendency to believe that there is something sacred and unalterable in these past achievements, and hence they are worshipped as "universal truths," not to be touched or questioned. The weight, accumulations and inertia of the past is immense, and continues to dictate what is supposed to be "moral," "normal," natural and "real".

A sad example of this authoritarian contamination from the past is the influence of the Old Testament on Christianity. The Presence and the New Tidings of the Christ are radically different and discontinuous from the old Hebrew tradition and law. No more "an eye for an eye," revenge, retribution, and extermination of enemies (the "unchosen"), but pure, unconditional Divine Love, Infinite Compassion, Forgiveness, and Peace!

Unfortunately, the history of Christianity has been a process of progressive contamination of the original Celestial Flame (described in the Gospels, especially St, John's) by the old scriptures, ancient laws and an overload of absurd, crazy-making dogmas and doctrines. The eternally New "Light of the World" shines afresh into each and all sacred Hearts, rekindling the Flame of Celestial Love!

After Saint Paul woke up to the Presence of Christ-Consciousness, he clearly stated: "When you are inspired and led by the Spirit (of the Risen Christ), you are no longer under the (old) law" (Galatians 5:18)

TIMELESS NOW

"You are an eternal being, now, on the pathway of
endless unfoldment. There is something within you
that sings the song of Eternity" – Ernest Holmes

From the Eastern doctrine of Avatars to the Western, Christian doctrine of the Incarnation of the Logos, there is the One, archetypal Idea that Celestial Beings become earthly individuals. And there seems to be a hierarchy of these divine Beings assuming a terrestrial embodiment. At the top are the bright stars, the founders of all main religions. Then, in descending order, their "apostles," disciples, followers and believers. But this monarchical, hierarchical, aristocratic, caste-like structure of "ranks" and degrees and states, has been (and continues to be), challenged by the radical democratic Realization of all Mystics, East and West. The Mystical-metaphysical view states that regardless of appearances, each individual human being is in essence otherworldly, an incarnation, projection or "ray" of the One, infinite, timeless Self. Every-one is an "avatar," an emissary from a star. Each Being is a beam, a "color," and there are exuberant hues between Light and Darkness. Each Soul *is* celestial!

This is why the Gita has been called "The Song Celestial," a reminder that the Atman-Self at the core-essence of each Heart and Soul is timeless, totally untouched and unaffected by worldly conditions. This Realization is the common ground; the "ground Luminosity" of all mysticism. It is indeed, a great paradox, as there is only One, infinite Self, yet myriad unique, individualizations of it. The other amazing paradox is the awakening of the dual self-consciousness of a distinct ego who strives to become its true self? The struggle, the quest, the effort, the hard work to finally become one's true self, when essentially we already, as ever, *are* that self that we long to become! We hear, again and again "trust thyself," "Be Yourself," "just Be who you are," etc., but the awakening of our distinct individuality/personality happens in a socio-cultural world of "becoming." There is the expectation and the pressure to be seriously involved in becoming someone. All manner of education, training, learning, conditioning and work is strongly focused on achieving goals, on demonstrating or manifesting this or that, on becoming a particular type of person. Only through some kind of accomplishment we are recognized, accepted and appreciated as "someone," yet those Great Souls, Heroes, Mahatmas, Saints and Geniuses that we look up to, brought significant world changes out of their Awakened Beingness. And whatever great "doing" happened, it was spontaneous, super-natural!

INTUITION – THE HEART'S INTELLIGENCE

Intuition is a direct knowingness from the heart. Another name for it is "telepathy," meaning "feeling at a distance." "Feeling" itself has a triple meaning: sensation, emotion and intuition ("gut-feeling"). The concept of "distance" implies physical separation, small or large. Another meaning for telepathy (*tele-pathos*) is "suffering at a distance" – deeply related to compassion – the awareness of suffering.

Esoteric, Initiatic and spiritual sciences speak about the awakening of the Heart's Intelligence as the next stage in the evolution of consciousness. This points to the re-awakening of intuition at a higher level, or turn of the spiral. Ancient and primitive cultures show a preponderance of intuitive knowledge of the inner and outer Kosmos. The advance of civilization, progress, industrialization and "electronization" relies heavily on reason, quantification, calculation and on overall mechanization of consciousness. The brain rules as the seat of intelligence, as the "Central Intelligence Agency," as the supreme "master-mind" and "control-room." The whole of our global Politics, Economy, Science and technology is a reflection of this "mechanization of consciousness." This brings to mind a painting by Goya entitled: "The dreams of Reason produces Monsters." And these obvious "monsters" show up as sophisticated and terrible weapons; as ecological contamination and destruction; as exploitation for profit; and as social injustice, poverty, hunger and the collective misery of millions. Hopefully, like the shadow side of adolescence, this is a temporary stage of human evolution.

Certainly, there are many indications that this global "madness" is being transcended, healed, trans-formed and superseded by a New, wholistic, Kosmic Consciousness. From the spiritual awakening of literally millions of individuals across the planet, to the creation of groups, associations, and organizations of all scales, from local to international, there seems to be a dawning, widespread awareness that a breakthrough in consciousness is indeed underway! And this trans-formation and breakthrough entails the awakening (or re-awakening) of the Heart's Intelligence, which is Intuition, Love, Compassion and Telepathy in its wider sense.

The spiritual awakening of Heart-consciousness involves a significant polarity, a double opening of the individual soul to the "collective unconscious" on the deeper side, and to the "collective superconscious" on the higher domain. Opening to the depths of our humanity we realize the vastness of suffering, physical, and psychological, from hunger, misery and violence, to grief, fear and anger. Our personal shadow opens up to the collective shadow of "the human condition," all daily reported in the news and global media. But, thank god, there is a simultaneous, complementary opening to the heights of the "collective superconscious," also called the Oversoul or the "Atmansphere."

Through prayer, adoration, meditation, contemplation and many other spiritual, trans-formative practices, the Heart-Soul opens up to the Celestial Light and Love. And this Influx from Higher Beings and Kingdoms has a tremendous Healing, Redeeming, Trans-muting and miraculous Power, at all levels. For instance, grief, sorrow, sadness and depression are transmuted into healing compassion, care and loving-kindness. Terror, fear, anxiety, panic and worry are trans-formed into total trust, faith and Reliance on Kosmic Goodness and Divine Providence. And the madness-energies of anger, hatred, aggression, violence and all destructive impulses and behaviors, are re-directed into creative channels; into the forces of integration, cooperation, synthesis, harmony and unity.

This simultaneous opening to Higher Worlds and Lower realms; to Above and Below; to Heaven and to "Hell" (mostly human created), is also a meeting; a blending and merging, an alchemical transubstantiation of both Kosmic Realms into the "Body of Glory;" the Body of Christ, the embodiment of the Holy Spirit in the Fire of Heart-Consciousness! And this Sacred Fire *is* Love, pure Love, evolving Love, Divine Love! And the tremendous miraculous, New-clear, Kosmic energy of Love, supernaturally neutralizes and transforms all darkness and density into Evolutionary Fuel! A new, fresh, Radiant Intuition; Luminous Intelligence, and transcendental Telepathy shines Bright from the core of the Blossoming Heart!

GRACE AND GRATITUDE

In Latin languages words that refer to grace (*gracia, gratia*), and words pointing to thankfulness or gratitude (*gracias*) are practically the same. There is also a third meaning attached to these words, and that is "gracefulness." This concept is associated with being delightful, pleasing, beautiful, uplifting, and even "funny (*gracioso*)."

Grace, as a divine, Kosmic, celestial gift, is not something given to some and withdrawn from others, but a universal, omnipresent Energy, Power, Substance ("food") or Emanation (from "Heaven") ever-available and totally accessible by each and all. How is it then that there seems to be a great variety of people in the spectrum of being graced to being disgraced? This amazing Karmic diversity related to grace does not mean that some enjoy an abundance of it while others are experiencing lack of it, privation and poverty. Grace is *not* like money or limited resources, it is already fully and ever-present, in its totality everywhere, within and without every-one.

The differences and variations reside in the capacity, potential, and ability of each unique being to draw, assimilate, utilize, embody and demonstrate (or express) grace, already and as-ever omnipresent; already celestially given. Increasing awareness of this "fullness of grace," (already bestowed or granted on, and as our beingness) spontaneously unfolds as gratitude. A tremendous exuberance of Life, Light and Love already exists in, through and all about us. We are already immersed in, and suffused by, this celestial ocean of grace! Glimpses into this truth blossom into feelings of thankfulness, joy, plenitude and generosity. An ever-fresh Fountain of Gratitude (for the Kosmic/Divine Cornucopia of gifts and blessings ceaselessly given) overflows the Heart's grail as rivers of compassion, service and care for all beings. The process of awakening to the "Amazing Grace" of Infinite Space; to the glorious, omnipresent Abundance of Beauty, Goodness and Love in the universe is the blessed Realization that as Kosmic Beings all that we could possibly need, in truth, we already have; we are already soaked through with It; we actually *are* It! In our quintessence we *are* grace-full, gracious and grateful! We *are* carriers of the Holy Grail!

Those Beings that we admire; that we look up to as "Great Souls" (Heroes, Saints, Geniuses), are the ones who realized themselves as embodiments of grace; as Holy, Wholesome and Wealthy instruments of Celestial Abundance! Their greatness, magnanimity and sacred nobility reside in their ability to receive and give *all*; to Be totally open to the Kingdom, the Power and the Glory, and let it flow as evolutionary Service to all beings.

Grace is in the air, in the light, in the waters, in all elements and energies, already suffusing and animating all celestial and terrestrial realms. The essence of gratitude is the re-cognition, appreciation and realization of the inherent Goodness of it *all*; of Existence; of Kosmic Reality; of *Being* It-Self! It is the awakening to the Plenitude and "Plenty-tude" of this ever-new Creation/ Evolution ceaselessly unfolding as exuberantly diverse lives.

The Immaculate, Radiant Heart of the Mother is indeed, "full of grace" (*gratia plena*) and it is continuously overflowing and outpouring Celestial gifts for every single one. Those aware and awake receive It all with a sacred *yes*! Becoming thus, Fountains of Benedictions for souls and worlds!

WHO KNOWS WHAT IS HAPPENING?

As I extend my subtle antennae into space, in the process of meditation and attunement with the sacred universe, I feel more and more that a tremendous "sea-change" is underway! Indeed, "The times they are a-changing!" as Bob Dylan announced, but in a much more profound and radical way than we dare to envision or imagine!

Indications from many sources bring glimpses into this awesome trans-formation in progress. Nature, the whole planet, the Cosmos, extraterrestrial and intraterrestrial influences and forces are certainly and actively at work!

The Earth as a Being is spontaneously responding to "civilization's" pressures, and as a macroorganism its "immune system" is counteracting a widespread "infection" brought about by human "germs" and "viruses." These "viruses" are more psychological than biological. They are mental-cultural belief systems based on a crystallization, hardening, petrification or "literarization" of consciousness. This we call "dogmatism," "fanaticism," "extremism," "fundamentalism," "scientism," etc. And it is a most dangerous rigidification of the mind into "black and white" thinking; a severe polarization of consciousness into "either-or," "us and them," generating paranoia and all manner of "enemies."

Weather patterns, climate change, natural upheavals, and man-made disasters are all indicating serious changes happening.

And all this is reflected in the mirror of the cybersphere, with its trillions of data and images, moment to moment "in the air."

What is this world-wide electronic "cloud of unknowing" revealing? A tremendous flux and circulation of all kinds of information and "messages" linking billions of people. These "horizontal" tidal waves of ceaseless media, data, messages and information seem helpful at many levels as it provides "access" and transparency. But at the same time, this "cloud" is actually blocking the higher and deeper Lights of Heaven and Earth.

"Vertically" piercing through this dark and heavy cloud-cover of the cybersphere are the rays of mystical/spiritual consciousness, that reconnect each Heart and Soul with the higher Noosphere and the "Atmansphere," that is, with an all-permeating Celestial Intelligence.

Who truly knows what is really going on? Those who are awake to the Kosmos; those whose consciousness is no longer entranced by the so-called "real" world of facts and figures; those who re-member themselves as offspring of the Universal Oversoul; those whose Hearts are open and blossoming in the Radiance of the Solar-Logos; those who have joined the Great School of Bodhisattvas and Mahatmas; those in fine harmonic resonance with the Celestial Power of Love!

THREE DARK CLOUDS

There are three main ideas, theories or mental constructs that tend to block the simple, pure truth of our inherent goodness, wholeness and fundamental perfection of Being.

1. The "Big Bang Theory," which assumes the existence of a "beginning;" the "objective" reality of time, space and energy; and the universe as purely "material," atomic, nuclear or "just chemistry."
2. The "Original Sin" theory, construct or belief, that assumes human consciousness to be a mistake; a falling away from a heavenly harmony; a basic, radical flaw in need of redemption or fixing.
3. The profoundly conditioned, or imprinted idea that being a human being *is* to be imperfect. All manner of socio-cultural feedback, since infancy, has again and again emphasized the message that there "*must*" be something wrong with us; something deficient, something in need of correcting, improving or rehabilitating.

How do these three deeply ingrained abstract theories or mental constructs obscure the realization of our true nature? The first answer is that early guilt and shame establish the foundations of feeling unworthy and not deserving due to some intrinsic "badness." You are not essentially good, that is the message, but you can and must try to "become" good in order to conform with others' expectations and "commandments."

To neutralize and "vaporize" these dark, heavy clouds we can recapture, re-member and rediscover our true, pristine, aboriginal nature; our inherent wholeness, beauty, perfection, goodness and wholesomeness; our fundamental soundness and sanity. And this *is* possible through the basic practices of meditation, prayer, adoration, and contemplation.

And as soon as we make real sense of Christ's statement about "being perfect as our Heavenly Father," then it begins to dawn on us that this "perfection," this quintessential wholeness is not something to "achieve," we *are* already that! But, of course, this ab-original wholeness and perfection does not apply to our conditioned ego-personality, bound to time and space. This spiritual evolution returning to our Heavenly Perfection may take innumerable reincarnations. And here is one of the greatest paradoxes; that we are involved in the immense process of ever-becoming the one, that in essence we eternally *are*, the Kosmic Self or Atman.

In the awakening process of re-membering our true "Buddha Nature," and realizing that in truth we *are* a precious Individualization of Infinite-Archetypal Harmony, Beauty, Love, Goodness, Light and Delight, we become liberated from "sin," shame, guilt and all accumulations of traumatic experiences and feedback. Realizing our essential agelessness or "beginninglessness" it becomes dazzlingly clear that no-one and no-thing (including the Whole Cosmos) ever began "once upon a time." It is *all,* ever-beginning/ending this very Infinite Moment!

THE MOST INFLUENTIAL

*"The deeper the self-realization of a human being, the
more he or she influences the whole universe by subtle
(sublime, divine) spiritual vibrations (emanations)
and the less he or she is affected by the phenomenal
flux." – Sri Yukteswar*

Who are the most spiritually influential human
beings on Earth today? Who are those whose
actual Presence on the Planet is uplifting,
positive, healing, pacifying, creative and illuminating? Not
politicians, billionaires, celebrities or those considered famous
or powerful by the media. Yes, these people spotlighted in the
news may have considerable influence in the lives of millions, but
mostly at low material levels, and even at dark and destructive
levels, such as war. Of course, some famous Luminaries such
as Mother Theresa, Mandela, Gorbachev, the Dalai Lama and
many others, are both well-known and carriers of very high,
luminous, enlightening influences affecting Humankind. But
there are literally millions of little known and unknown souls,
all over the Earth, that are shining, emanating highly positive
energies and vibrating in harmonic resonance with Heaven.
Through their uplifting, trans-formative, Radiant selves, the
world *is* changed, and through their influence upon the Collective
Conscious and Unconscious, evil and darkness are counteracted

and neutralized, and the Celestial influences of the Oversoul or Collective Superconscious (Communion of Saints or Mahatma sphere) are channeled and grounded on Earth as Healing Peace and Higher Consciousness.

Any-one (in any household, community, village, town, city, or country) whose soul opens up to the ever-present glory of this sacred/miraculous universe, can become significantly influential in the overall enlightening of humanity. Just by embodying higher Life, Light and Love; just by "being the change," just by Realizing the Self, they exert a tremendous, truly powerful, yet super-subtle influence on millions of other beings.

Crossing the threshold of death, the angels will be delighted to show us who the true "stars" are! But we can become one right now by awakening the sacred splendor of our own souls, by Realizing our quintessential Celestial Nature! As we remember ourselves as stars "on assignment" on Earth, as Holy Flames of pure Love, then our very Presence is greatly beneficial and influential. Thus we are super-naturally drawn to "birds of a feather;" to loved ones, friends and coworkers (disciples and masters).

THE SUPERCONSCIOUS

As the first half of the 20th century was a time of
discovery and rediscovery of the Unconscious, both
personal and collective, (through the work of Freud,
Jung and many others), so the beginning of the 21st century (and
3rd millennium) is the opening up of the Superconscious. Of
course, great Initiates and Mahatmas, such as Rudolf Steiner,
Vivekananda, Aurobindo, Omraam Mikhaël Aïvanhov and
several other spiritual luminaries, were already unveiling the
realms of superconsciousness last century.

The Supramental, Divine and Cosmic aspects of consciousness
were always the domain of the Mystics; the revelations of the
Timeless, Perennial Wisdom, but right now this morphogenetic
field of Higher Consciousness (the Mahatmasphere or Noosphere)
is becoming increasingly intense and luminous. Its shadow aspect
is the Cybersphere saturating the electronic "air", and making
enormous amounts of information widely available. But the
vibrant omnipresence of the Mahatmasphere is making Cosmic
consciousness instantly accessible and available to any soul finely
attuned to it. This Super-conscious Realm is also "collective" as
it includes The Light and Love of innumerable celestial Brothers
and Sisters; of a whole Hierarchy of Higher and Divine Beings.
The personal or individualized Superconscious is what has been
called "Higher Self," Soul, Psychic Being, or Individuality. It is
the celestial aspect or dimension of the self which assumes a body

and personality in each incarnation in order to undergo a specific Karmic/Dharmic work.

The collective superconscious constitutes a diverse and exuberant community of Beings; a complex and colorful spectrum of many degrees of cosmic consciousness, a vast and immense Hierarchy, terrestrial and celestial. It includes a whole range of Saints, Initiates, Mahatmas, Paramhansas, all the way to the realm of Avatars or Divine Incarnations. In a simultaneous and parallel and cosmic dimension there are the "Celestial Intelligences," from Angels and Archangels to Cherubim and Seraphim, an immense variety of devas weaving and working through innumerable Kingdoms. The Atman within each and all is the link between the personal and the collective superconscious, the space or sacred dimension where "singular" and "plural" are One. For spiritual, evolutionary purposes, the important point is that as individual, embodied, human beings we already have the potential and capacity to syntonize or harmonize with the Atman sphere; with the omnipresent Realm of cosmic/divine Superconsciousness. Through prayer, contemplation and meditation we can instantly access and partake with the grace of Higher Kingdoms.

THE ERA OF THE NOOSPHERE

We have indeed entered a new era of planetary consciousness, called by many the "Noosphere" (see Appendix I). This is a sphere of human thinking, knowledge, awareness and ultimately "cosmic consciousness" that surrounds and infuses the whole Earth. What is called the "Cybersphere" (the global layer or "cloud" of electronic communication enveloping the planet) is but a pale reflection of the actual Noosphere, which essentially is trans-rational, telepathic, supramental and mystical, or in other words, instantaneous, simultaneous, synchronous and "non-local."

The fact that any individual with the right gadget (computer, phone, etc.) is able to access a tremendous amount of information, knowledge, or data on any subject is a crude metaphor of the actual human capabilities, faculties, and potentials to directly access higher and deeper dimensions of consciousness, the "Akasha" or cosmic "morphogenetic fields" of celestial consciousness. This is precisely what Mystics, Saints, Initiates, Visionaries, Prophets and "awakened souls" have done, and continue to do, all across the planet.

The Noosphere, like the atmosphere surrounding the Earth, has many levels. It is a whole spectrum of awareness, consciousness, illumination, and Realization. At the "infrared" level, metaphorically speaking, there is the increasingly common awareness of a lot going on affecting peoples, cultures, and the whole planetary ecology. Of course, the media, communication, and the cybersphere play a role here. But this awareness goes beyond mere information, as people are experiencing directly "climate change" and other changes and shifts in the natural, socio-cultural worlds.

At the middle and higher levels, the Noosphere becomes more "vertical," celestial and divine, and less "horizontal," terrestrial and merely human. There is also an increasing "harmonic resonance" with the exuberant diversity of further evolved noospheres unfolding simultaneously across billions of galaxies. Innumerable planet-worlds evolving life and consciousness *seem* at first cosmically isolated, unique, weird, or a freak phenomenon (as Earth dwellers tend to think), but in truth, nothing and no one is really isolated in the Cosmos.

As migratory birds and insects crisscross our planet, seeding and pollinating biodiversity across the Earth, so there are myriad evolving souls migrating (or "trans-migrating") across countless worlds, carrying and sharing the subtle seeds of celestial consciousness. These spiritual "messengers" constitute the Hierarchies, both planetary and celestial, that are ever-facilitating the exchange and circulation of Higher Consciousness among myriad unfolding noospheres. What do Avatars, Angels, and "Aliens" have in common? They are all "weavers" of "Immense Intelligence;" composers, conductors and players in the ever-unfolding Symphony of Creation/Evolution; divine Artists playing with and displaying the infinite colors and harmonies of Consciousness.

Earth and Humanity are now at the critical, crucial stage of Noospheric development in which there is an increasing awareness of the "Messengers'" Presence. We may call them deities, bodhisattvas, Avatars, Angels, Extra-Terrestrials, Mahatmas, Spirits, Entities, Beings of Light, etc. They seem to be carriers or embodiments of very high ("ultraviolet") levels of cosmic consciousness, and they are here to stir up our awareness and cosmic memory of the sacred-celestial nature of our very souls, the Earth, and "all sentient Beings!"

ENVISIONING

*"We undergo the development (evolution, unfoldment,
advancement, blossoming) we envision for ourselves;
we get the evolution we deserve"* – *Theodor Roszak*

This quote applies both individually and collectively. How do I see or envision my evolutionary possibilities and potentialities? Here is where the great blocks, obstacles and hindrances lie: the personal, social and cultural assumptions of what is possible to become. But those who manage to break through all manner of false consensus about what is truly Real and Possible, soon discover (re-discover) a universe teeming with miraculous possibilities. And I have come to experience glorious glimpses into the sacred Kosmos boiling with awesome, celestial, exuberant and tremendous possibilities.

This I have seen through three main portals and openings. One is the actual lives and works of Great Souls (Mahatmas, Paramhansas, Initiates, Saints). Another is through the wondrous displays, wisdom, and Beauty of Nature and the Universe; the incredible exuberance and diversity of Life across the immensity of space. Worlds upon worlds, Kingdoms, Realms, Dimensions… And the third, or other door opening to the unfathomable glory of Being, is into the very Heights and Depths of my own Self, this Soul or individualized Spirit I *am*! And this Celestial Beingness that I re-discover *in* and *as* myself, is profoundly linked to and inter-dependent with the Beingness of Heaven and Earth, and with all souls across the worlds.

As Terence remarked that nothing human could be alien to him, so I add that nothing subhuman or natural, or nothing superhuman or celestial is alien to me either. I exist, thrive, evolve, and unfold in a cosmic sea of souls, Kingdoms Above and Below ever-interpenetrating and nurturing each-other. So, I now know intuitively or have a luminous Idea of my evolutionary possibilities; of who I could become, because I have seen the golden seeds within, and I have felt the Holy Flame in my Heart of hearts. But mostly because the quintessence of who I am, this Celestial Self, is already, as ever, Good, Perfect, Sublime, and Divine as the whole is! Indeed, I am a unique, precious expression and embodiment of Infinite Wellbeing, and so is every-one; every single human being! To Be is to partake and share with all Beingness; with innumerable souls among the stars; with all Hearts, dim or bright, across the infinite, sacred Night!

MYSTICISM AND THE FUTURE OF EARTH

There have never been so many mystics alive on this planet as today. And these contemporary Mystics are becoming increasingly articulated, creative and resourceful at expressing and formulating the exuberant "colors" of consciousness. And not only a new language is emerging, a brilliant blend of prose and poetry; of science and art; of a higher Reason and an uplifted Imagination, but also, and most significantly, a new way of Being in the World. Because true Mysticism is trans-denominational and profoundly experiential, it is free from dogmas, doctrines or formalized beliefs (Religions, Philosophies, etc.), and it is deeply grounded in Kosmic Reality.

Individual Mystics are truly upright, noble, profoundly attuned with Heaven and Earth, "vertically" in-tune with "what is really going on!" Hence, in the Big Picture, they are the most practical, effective and influential people on the planet. Real Mystics are not otherworldly dreamers out of touch with what is happening on Earth today.

What the media daily reports as "breaking news" is not only a one-sided distortion, but also a tiny fragment of what is really and truly happening across the whole world, and through innumerable souls.

The Mystic's Heart is truly inclusive, vast, all-comprehending, in other words: Kosmic, both open to Infinite Compassion and to "Eternal Delight."

Aware of the unspeakable suffering of human and other sentient beings upon the Earth, the true Mystic fully embodies the Power and the Presence of Celestial Love, and engages all his or her faculties, gifts and talents towards alleviating, reducing or trans-forming all manner of pain. In this "Bodhisattva" endeavor or service, great joy and enthusiasm radiates from the core of Beingness.

On the contrary, half-baked mystics become detached, melancholic, disengaged, otherworldly and self-preoccupied, in other words, narcissistic. On the other extreme there are the blind, practical, "realistic," down-to-business people obsessed with doing, or "getting things done," mainly for profit, power or pleasure. Then there are the rebels, radicals and activists fighting back structures and hierarchies; corporations and governments; economic and political systems. These "freedom fighters" for social justice, against ecological destruction and the general insanity of civilization can also be "half-baked" mystics stuck on acting and reacting always "against" something, and not rooted or centered in the "vertical" dimension that truly reveals the Big Picture of "what is really going on."

Real change, true trans-formation is centrifugal, from within outwards. "Be the change you envision for the world" as Gandhi proposed. Become the ideal in your Heart. Be who you really are. "Manifest the divinity within you and everything will rearrange itself around it" – Said Vivekananda.

This is the great work—(opus magnum) of the Real Mystic who becomes "a living Flame of Love" (Saint John of the Cross) or a "Sacred Activist" (according to Andrew Harvey), truly effective and efficient because "vertically" attuned with the Spirit Above and Below, Celestial and terrestrial.

A "horizontal" survey of the state of the world, from all angles, ecological, political, economic, humanitarian, military, and all manner of global crises, tend to present a bleak picture of the future. Form global warming to weapons proliferation, to overpopulation and famine, and other imbalances, the overall forecast is indeed pretty disturbing. But, why is it that real mystics are also "optimystics"? Because in their profound perception, vision, and realization of the truly Big Picture, all is well, all seeming chaos included. And in the words of Julian of Norwich: "All shall be well, and all manner of things shall be well." This is not a naïve, blind statement, but an articulation of a mystical, "vertical" Realization that in the Kosmic context all is indeed in Divine Order. We exist in a miraculous universe, and wondrous trans-formations *are* possible!

> *"True and genuine mysticism springs from the capacity*
> *to have Imaginations, to receive impressions from Higher*
> *Worlds, and to articulate them by means of the Heart's*
> *Intelligence. Mystical experiences, like intellectual experiences,*
> *must become the common heritage of humankind."*

Rudolf Steiner

ALWAYS... YET

Always the search, the longing
of the Beloved for the Beloved,
and yet they are one in the vast sea of the soul.
Always the adventure, the quest
for the effulgent grail and the grace,
yet, their splendor
shines daily from our Sun.
Always the inquiry and the questions
for origins and beginnings,
and yet the one cause is ever-now
in the infinite Present that is.
Always the riddle and the mystery
of arriving and departing.
and yet the Heart remembers
ceaseless, celestial journeys.

CHAPTER 5

TRANS-FORMATION DOWN TO EARTH

THREE MENTAL "VIRUSES"

As there are biological microorganisms that cause all manner of diseases, and electronic "viruses" that generate distortions and chaos, so there are also mental viruses. The three most insidious and nefarious are: "only one," "nothing but," and "forever."

1. The "only one," or "mono" mental virus is characterized by the negation of diversity and the insistence that there is "only one." Examples of the pernicious influence of this virus are: monotheism, monopoly, monogamy, monoculture, and many other "monos." It is a manic-obsessive tendency, or fixation on an idea that includes all manner of fundamentalism. It is a "seizure" or crystallization of thinking that prevents alternatives, variety, pluralism, multiplicity and diversity. It is a rigid, inflexible, dogmatic attitude that generates untold human suffering.

2. Another deleterious mental virus is the one that creates the tendency to explain all manner of phenomena as "nothing but" this or that. It is also called reductionism. Instances of this include statements such as: "The universe is nothing but the accidental collocation of atoms" (as Bertrand Russel would say), or "Consciousness is nothing but the electrochemistry of the brain," or "Life is nothing

but the outcome of complex molecules," etc. This attitude affects all areas of culture reducing even the highest manifestations of the human spirit to "nothing but" sublimations of the basic survival instincts. This virus tends to reduce archetypes into black and white stereotypes, and whatever is considered sublime, sacred, ideal or divine into the lowest possible common denominator. It is a "flattening" of Reality and a denial of the Hierarchy of Kingdoms. All is "nothing but" the effervescent interplay of subatomic particles!

3.   A third destructive virus produces the mental attitude, or delusion of "forever," or "always the same," or "permanence." This is a defensive denial of the reality of change, flux and impermanence. This has been also called "monumentalism," the belief that certain laws or things remain "always the same," forever unchanged, "written in stone." Something fixed in the hoary past is determined forever and cannot be changed, from natural to supernatural "laws." Here again is rigidity, literalism and fundamentalism − the belief that certain truths or principles, or laws, remain "forever the same." There is no possible change or alternative to these divinely or cosmically ordained "iron laws" such as "scriptures", constitutions, and even the "laws of nature" or "constants," like gravity and the speed of light (now being realized to be not truly "constant" but fluctuating).

Are there any "antiviral medications" to counteract and neutralize these viruses? Yes there are!

As the common features of these three mental viruses are: contraction, closure, rigidity and hardening or "freezing," whatever helps with expansion, opening, flexibility, softening and warming should work to neutralize or transmute these viruses. For instance, to counteract the "mono" virus, an expanded imagination, to include the multicolor spectrum of Diversity, Multiplicity, Variety and Pluralism, could facilitate transcending the fixation on the "only one."

To overcome the Reductionism of the "nothing but" virus, a "vertical" opening to the "Great Chain of Being" or the Hierarchy of Kingdoms can help with the realization that there are indeed innumerable worlds, realms and dimensions. Not only "matter" shows many different levels of complexity, but also Life manifests through all manner of Kingdoms. And further still, Consciousness in the universe displays an exuberant spectrum of domains.

Regarding the "forever" virus, the best antidote is the Buddhist Idea and Realization of "Impermanence," that nothing and no-one remains the same; that all forms are transitory; and that there is a continuous cosmic flow of trans-formation going on!

"Thanks to impermanence anything is possible"

Thich Nhat Hanh

CRACK OF DAWN

Throughout the turmoil, struggles, conflicts and upheavals of current world events, there are glimmerings of awakening. The nightmare is real enough for very many human beings in terrible situations, but because now there is an increasing transparency, the truth of what is really going on shines more and more, in spite of all the cunning strategies of deceits and propaganda. Violence is what it is, a destructive behavior, and all the justifications and euphemisms in the world shall not succeed in obscuring the fact that Peace, Harmony, Cooperation and Common Sense cannot be realized through the opposite means of war, discord, conflict, violence and dogmatism.

Fundamentalism, personal or collective, religious, political, economic, military, private or public, is a kind of subtle seizure of the brain; a crystallization of thinking; a psychic or mental virus that tends to freeze the mind into black and white concepts; a mechanization of logic into a strict duality; a rigidification or petrification of consciousness into literalism; the breakdown of true intelligence into cleverness, cunning, slyness, machinations and all the strategies of deceit.

But all this madness and darkness is now being infiltrated and irradiated by kosmic/celestial beams of a Higher consciousness. The Luminous, sharp, sacred rays of Saint Michael, other Archangels, and many other Heavenly Beings (Bodhisattvas) are piercing through the dark density of the "dragon." The "monster" of materialism, consumerism, denial of the sacred, and the pursuit of sheer power, profit and pleasure, is being neutralized and transmuted by "The Light of the World;" by the Radiance of the Risen Christ, and by the Presence of Maitreya – the kosmic Buddha of Infinite Light and Compassion!

In this new dawn of consciousness, this fresh Celestial Light is more and more difficult to hide, to cover up, to pretend, to lie. As the "table top" becomes increasingly translucent and transparent, all "under the table," covert, secret, classified, dark operations become exposed. The nightmare still lingers over the planet, but the crack of a new dawn brings true hope and an increasing clarity of our true evolutionary Purpose.

> *"The world is all right; it is not going to hell, on the contrary,*
> *it is getting good so fast that in the process many things are*
> *being overturned & confusion appears to be on the surface, as*
> *we have become hypnotized by a few strong-minded people.*
>
> *But underneath, the ever-Creative Power is*
> *at work dissolving all unlike itself."*

Ernest Holmes

CONSCIOUS ALIGNMENT

"It is our purpose and destiny to bring (or open up) a
new dimension into this world by living in conscious
alignment with Universal Intelligence" (Infinite
Divine Order) – Eckhart Tolle

How do we know when we are aligned or out of tune? The awareness of dissonance, friction, struggle, dis-ease, dis-order, frustration, resistance, pain, confusion, turmoil or "noise" is an indication that something is "out of whack;" that there is a discrepancy or misalignment in some aspect of our life. On the contrary, when we become aware of Harmony, alignment or fine attunement with the Divine and dynamic Kosmic Order or Intelligence, there is a threefold experience and realization:

1. There is the Presence of vibrant joy and vitality; enthusiasm and well-being, true Peace and Strength.
2. There is the Presence of a sublime Warmth, Love, care and compassion for all beings, Kosmic Empathy!
3. There is the Presence of Light, clarity, vision, comprehension, insight, inspiration and illumination.

And these "Presences" are not only Energies or states of consciousness, but also the Presence of Beings, Celestial visitors; angels and divine entities, inhabitants of the Invisible Worlds who are responding to our invocations and invitations!

HOMEWORK

In the school of life those who neglect to do their "homework" tend to fail or "de-grade" more rapidly. We are all familiar with the concept and purpose of academic homework as extra practice, study, review, and preparation. This applies to all manner of learning: subjects, skills, instruments, languages, etc.

Education in general includes theoretical and practical knowledge aimed at providing functional and eventually professional skills for all kinds of specialized "doing." But Self-Knowledge, which includes the development of deeper and higher levels of awareness and consciousness, is not emphasized or expected. It is left as a personal, private matter, like spirituality or therapy.

The importance of having an active and rich "inner life;" of engaging in regular "inner work;" of developing the "intrapersonal," "existential" and spiritual "intelligences" is now, more and more, being realized at large. But still, only the Few are aware of the cosmic significance of actually "doing your Homework;" of being involved in a daily spiritual, metaphysical or sacred practice; of "working on oneself" and being in tune with the many domains of the Self.

Most people use all their time and energy for surviving purposes. Those better off fill the gap with "leisure" and "entertainment." Why wait till the Physician, the Judge, the Psychotherapist, the Priest, or the very Angel of Death reminds us of our neglect? Let's take care now of our *real homework*! (See Appendix II)

KOSMIC ASSIMILATION

At times, when my Heart-Consciousness opens up to the awesome omnipresence of grace, I realize, ever afresh, the Reality of a perpetual, perennial, Influx of sacred, celestial Energy. This ceaseless inflow or downpour of Divine, Kosmic forces, emanations and elements is ever-coming from our sun – the Solar Logos – and from innumerable other suns and worlds bringing ever-new influences to our planet from the unfathomable depths of space. And this very constant infusion of the Celestial Powers of Pure Love, Pure Light, and Pure Life, *is* the Infinite Mother, ever sustaining us, nurturing us and protecting us from inner and outer darkness. Indeed, it is protecting Earth and Humanity from its own dangerous delusions; from the insanity of "civilization;" from all the "isms" of the world; from self-destruction.

One aspect of this continuous Influx of Sacred Energy is the Kosmic Power of Peace – which is Divine Order, Harmony, Beauty, Light and True Intelligence. And this ever-descending *pax plena* is being embodied in rocks, in trees, in warm hearts, the whole earth, and Luminous Souls. It is in all beings, natural and supernatural. And it shines through each and all uniquely and differently according to each one's opacity or transparency; to each one's degree of translucence. Saints, Mahatmas and Initiates are so because they have become conscious, willing, most loving and delightful "instruments of Peace." The Luminous Awareness of their open Hearts enables them to receive and give; to circulate these celestial currents; to be "organs of its activity and receivers of its truth" (Ralph Waldo Emerson); to absorb, assimilate and embody this Kosmic Glory, and let It radiate as benedictions and inspirations into others' stories!

The more I consciously breathe-in this ever-streaming *pax-prana*, *gratia plena* or *mare stellarum* (*ave maria*), the Holy Spirit of the Celestial Mother, the more Inspired I am; the more charged, fulfilled, energized and enthused to shine and share this "Best of time and space" flowing through! Alive, awake, and aflame within this vibrant omnipresence of Celestial *Life*, *Light* and *Love*, I delight in the practice of "*Kosmosis*," that is, the direct absorption of sacred, Kosmic energies and emanations. Thus, my "bodies" and their organs, functions, and faculties, naturally and supernaturally receive and transmit these sacred currents; these "Winds of Grace." Breathing-out, in thought, word, song and deed I bless my world and planet, and every single soul in my life! Amen!

REMEMBER SURRENDER

A t the root of restlessness, apprehension, fear, anxiety and all subtle and obvious paranoia is a deeply ingrained conditioning and belief that we exist in a very dangerous world, a hostile universe, a Kosmos that is continuously threatening us with extermination and extinction. This conviction, belief or inner attitude is constantly triggering our basic survival instinct, our readiness to resist, fight or escape from whatever is perceived as threatening our security.

We have to be protected, shielded, armored, covered, always prepared for "the worst case scenario". This is the way of defensiveness, mistrust, doubt, worry, nervousness, resistance, hostility, animosity, contraction and hardness. This is the attitude of stressing and struggling, of forcing and straining, of resisting and pushing, of saying <u>NO</u> to what is.

On the contrary, the universal message of the great Souls, (the Mahatmas, the Mystics, the great Initiates and spirits of all traditions, the Timeless Priests and Shamans, and the great Poets, Philosophers, Artists and Scientists of all times) is that we exist in a most loving and friendly universe, that the whole of Creation/Evolution is in truth our Celestial Mother, ever caring and nurturing our divine growth. As R. W. Emerson said: "We lie in the lap of Immense Intelligence, which makes us organs of its activity and receivers of its truth."

This means that we already exist as condensations, embodiments, or unique Individualizations of an immense, vast, profound, infinite Wisdom that we call Light, or Life, or Love! And, as embodied beings, one-of-a-kind expressions of this Celestial ocean of Intelligence, we are "organs of its activity," that is, channels, conduits or outlets of the fundamental Cosmic Creative Energy. And this ever-creative Power and Glory is ever-active *in*, *through*, and *as* each of its myriad individualizations.

Actually, all Beings of all Kingdoms are expressions of this exuberant Beauty, Goodness and Truth (even those which temporarily appear ugly, bad, evil, dark and deceitful). To be "receivers of its Truth" means to be cosmically designed and equipped to resonate in harmony with "The Music of the Infinite Celestial Spheres," to be able, and capable of the finest and highest attunement.

The complementary truth of the Mystics, Avatars, Paramhansas and Self-Realized Souls, is that we need to stop fighting and resisting what is, because this attitude is rejecting and saying no to the very "best of time and space;" to that which we are desperately longing for; Higher Love, Divine Light, Eternal Life. Our very fear, dread, mistrust, and defensiveness insulates us from Heaven, so that we become cut-off and isolated from the glory that is. Of course, this negative, dark attitude is an illusion, a temporary nightmare, as in truth it is impossible to be totally cut-off from Heaven. Even in Hell, or the darkest, densest realms, Celestial grace is Present!

So the core message of the Mystics is to surrender to the omnipresent goodness and Perfection that is! How do we learn to do this? First of all, in our fundamental nature as offspring of the Infinite, we already know it. We have trusted; we have totally relied on Providence, we have surrendered to Nature and the Universe countless times and lives before. Like falling asleep in out mother's bosom, or fully letting go in our lover's embrace, the experience of surrender is not something new or foreign to us. And second, we have been civilized, domesticated and conditioned as rational-intellectual beings, giving priority to our thinking heads over our feeling hearts. And in this process of "education" we have been programmed to believe in a blind, hostile, dead and dangerous universe. So, how can we surrender to chaos and randomness?

But, as we change our outlook, world-view and conception of Reality, and we begin to see and recognize Order, Purpose, Harmony and Intelligence across all cosmic dimensions, then we can trust again. Confidence, Faith, and Reliance on a higher-deeper Wisdom begins to irradiate our consciousness. And then, slowly but surely, our Heart starts to remember again how to relax "in the lap of Immense Intelligence"; how to surrender to the Infinite Divine! And so, relinquishing the illusion of "control" we rediscover with sublime delight that it is the Light that is taking care of all!

"And all shall be well and all manner of thing
shall be well." –Julian of Norwich

PRACTICING TRANSFIGURATION

"If you are not shining, the world is not benefited." –
Peter Ragnar

We are by nature already divinely designed to shine. Our soul's sacred core is already, as ever, Radiant and splendid as a sunrise. Its timeless Splendor is ever-glowing and spreading its inherent, essential Beauty, Truth and Goodness. Why isn't it obvious? Why do most people appear dull and dark? Can we experience this Radiance in others? And in our own selves? Yes we can. Aspects or glimpses of this Radiance show as the "glow" of pregnant mothers; as the beauty of babies and children in general; as the natural glow of love and delight shared by souls intimately in touch. It also manifests through the pristine beauty and spontaneity of indigenous, aboriginal people. And also through elders, glowing with Wisdom and Kindness. But most of all, this sacred Radiance shows up distinctly in the face, eyes and overall demeanor of evolved souls, saints, Initiates and Mahatmas. These are the Great Masters of Beauty, Truth and Goodness that we admire and venerate. Their mere Presence emanates and radiates Peace, Love, Wisdom, Strength and otherworldly Beauty. Their various "bodies" appeared transfigured by the Radiance of their auras; by their core-Splendor shining through.

At the sacred core of their Being, every soul already shines, but the layers, "bodies," veils or coverings surrounding the Aboriginal Flame vary in density, thickness, opacity or translucence. Also, our capacity to become aware of others' soul-glow is related to our own soul awareness, to our own "transparency to transcendence," which is "transparency to immanence," as well. As certain animals are equipped with infrared vision, so we can develop our "ultraviolet" vision, that is, our capacity to notice and perceive the Soul's splendor. Another name for this Radiance is "aura," and the more pure, luminous and strong its super-natural glow, the more beneficial its influence on others, and at the same time, the more protected from negative or dark influences. How to allow this splendor to manifest through our body, personality or presence? Can we "practice" transfiguration? Yes, first purely in our uplifted Imagination, but most importantly by the steady cultivation of virtues and by the ongoing purification/transmutation of our "bodies," and by releasing all past contaminations and surrender into the inherent Glory *that-is!*

"There is the same pure white light-an emission of the divine Being-in the center of each, but the glass being of different colors and thickness, the rays assume diverse aspects in the transmission. The quality and beauty of each central flame is the same, and the apparent inequality is only in the imperfection of the temporal instrument of its expression. As we rise higher and higher in the scale of being, the medium becomes more and more translucent."

Vivekananda

A MASTER-PIECE IN PROGRESS

W e are all working, consciously or unconsciously, in our unique Master-piece called "the body of glory." This ongoing project, ever in progress, we carry across many incarnations. This is the "Living Temple" or Tabernacle, where the divine can dwell and radiate forth its gifts to the world. Each particular physical/organic embodiment, or "life," is like a "scaffolding" that enables us to concentrate our creativity in an area of our "temple" or cathedral. But the overall "imprint" or plan, and the accomplished corners or "altars" we carry from one existence to another. Thus, whatever the situation or condition, we continue working on our unique "Master-piece ins progress," in our "body of glory," and the more consciously the better.

All truly creative "workshops" generate "messes," debris, dust, and seeming disorder or chaos. But increasing discernment or consciousness makes clear the difference between the work itself (as a manifestation of Beauty, Truth or Goodness) and all collateral confusion, dirt, or temporary mess. We all know that when there is construction, remodeling, fixing or painting going on, some measure of chaos and disorder is expected. We also know that the re-arrangement and change is temporary. The same with little children at play, exploration or experimentation. Mess is always part of it!

Similarly, in our evolutionary journey, exploration and living; and as we work on our "microcosmic Master-piece;" confusion, chaos, disorder and disorganization are part and parcel of the overall equation; the immense quest. Thus, our lives show a bright side of order, harmony, intelligence, integration and synthesis; and also a dark side or "shadow" full of mistakes, messes, misses (sins/stains) chaos and disintegration or breakdown. Kosmos and Compost; Light and Darkness; Beauty and the "Beast"!

All the great Masters, Mystics and Mahatmas shows us (as sublime Role Models) that what truly matters is to keep the focus on the Archetypal Ideal; to allow the higher guidance of Inspiration to propel our journey. Debris, dirt, dust, refuse, leftovers, litter and "garbage" (inner and outer) shall in due time be recycled, disposed or "composted." All the "bodies" in their formation and trans-formation require "assimilation" and "elimination," so does our "Body of Glory." Thus, we absorb the sacred and let go of the profane and mundane. We are ever-renewed in this blessed Kosmic circulation!

"WHAT GOES AROUND COMES AROUND"

This well-known popular saying is deeply rooted in the timeless Wisdom of Humanity, and has many levels of meaning. It expresses a two-foldness and a reciprocity or correspondence. The two aspects are: what goes out, whatever is sent, broadcasted, shared, exerted, radiated outwards, emanated, projected, etc. And what is encountered, met, received, taken-in, what happens, whatever or whoever comes our way. (Of course, this is profoundly connected with the famous and ancient Laws of Karma and Dharma).

The second aspect points to the reciprocal interconnection or interdependence between the two gestures or movements; between centrifugal and centripetal forces, vibrations and emanations. The various levels or layers of meaning illuminate the fact that this exchange, interaction or relationship is always at work and play; it is ceaselessly happening, yet the significant difference concerns the kind and quality of consciousness involved.

Whatever we are thinking, feeling or doing at any given moment, has multiple repercussions, obvious or subtle, within and without. The more conscious, sensitive or aware of this constant broadcast going on, the less victimized by fate or circumstances we feel, as we realize that we *do* have a choice regarding what "goes around," what we are sending or disseminating into the world. Thus we can gain a measure of control ("inner locus of control"), self-monitoring and self-awareness. We discover, more and more that we *can* think differently, change our emotions and direct our behaviors. And as we do, we shall soon realize that whatever or whoever is "coming around" has a different quality to it, a more luminous "color" or vibration.

We also realize that these two complementary aspects, what goes out and what comes in, can function either as a "vicious circle" or as a "virtuous spiral." The "vicious" or mechanical aspect consists in the feeling or belief of being stuck under the influence or power of circumstances – past or present situations. This is the hopeless experience that whatever is going on within (emotions, thoughts, actions), or without (others, situations) is totally out of our control. Here are the roots of fatalism, despair and hopelessness. But there exists the blessed possibility of breaking this iron ring of recurring negativity and disaster. This possibility has been given various names such as "grace," divine freedom, transcending the "Wheel of Karma," spiritual Awakening, breakthrough denial, a "quantum leap in consciousness," etc.

The essential point here is that the light of self-awareness can break this shackle or vicious circle, into an ascending spiral of healing, redemption, trans-formation and spiritual growth. And this inner-work of change, recovery, overcoming and wholesome development can be done by starting to work simultaneously on both sides of the equation. On the one side by becoming increasingly aware of "what is going around." What am I thinking? What kind of mood am I projecting? What am I doing? What kind of words am I throwing around? How do I feel on a daily basis? What kind of "vibes," emanations or energy am I broadcasting? And here we begin to realize that we have been conditioned, "educated," brought up or programmed to think, feel or behave as we do, but we *can* change all this!

On the other side of the equation – "what comes around" (whatever is happening or did happen), we can start to focus on all the good things, people and circumstances in our life. To "count our blessings" and realize more and more how amazingly graced we truly are. This will allow feelings of gratitude, joy and appreciation to unfold and blossom. Together with this increased feelings of thankfulness for this "amazing grace," ever flowing and circulating through our soul and world, the liberating feeling of forgiveness also unfolds. To truly forgive is to let go of all grudges, resentment, hatreds, rancor, guilt, shame, complaints, grievances and bad feelings regarding everyone, beginning with oneself!

And as we learn to send and receive greater and greater Beauty, Truth, and Goodness, or higher Love, Light, and Life. So do we ascend the sacred spiral of Evolution becoming a brighter and brighter star of benedictions to all.

MYSTICALLY IN TOUCH

When we become truly in touch and in tune with what is really going on in the unfathomable Kosmos, then we are in Harmony; at one with the ever-unfolding Perfection that-is. There is a "horizontal," superficial and artificial "going on" ceaselessly transmitted by the media, the cybersphere and all manner of information crisscrossing the planet. All this is what it seems to, or appears to be going on: trivia, terrorism, accidents, natural catastrophes, crime, scandals, war, contamination, etc. Chaotic and destructive events are indeed happening, but in the light of the Big Picture, they are a tiny, a very small fragment or "particle" of "what is Really going on" in the Universe, in the Heights and Depths of Heaven and Earth.

To become conscious, aware and attuned to this Kosmic Reality; to the glory and the immensity that-is, three basic fine-tunings are required: the profound harmonization of *the body, the mind* and *the Heart*.

It is important to remember that each of these aspects or domains has been already divinely designed and equipped to resonate with ultimate Reality, that is Infinite Life, Light and Love. Through all manner of body postures, attitudes, adjustments, gestures, inner and outer movements, stillness, sensations, manipulations, exercises and meditations, the living body can vibrate in harmonic resonance with Life, Universal Life, ever-creative Life, exuberant, Eternal Life!

Our precious human body is already a fantastic instrument, a cosmic "Stradivarius," celestially designed to vibrate with the timeless Music of Creation. Through what we call "the mind," our conscious rational, thinking domain, it is possible to be "in tune with the Infinite," in syntony with Universal Mind or "Mind at Large," also called "Immense Intelligence." This happens through the practice of Contemplation, uplifted Imagination, Creative Thinking, Intuition and the unfolding of supra-mental consciousness. Illumination is attunement with the omnipresent "Infinite Light," the "Solar Logos" or "Cosmic Consciousness."

Through the fine-tuning or sacred Resonance of the Heart, the Soul Re-members itself as a beam of Cosmic Love, infinite Compassion and "Eternal Delight." The Intelligence of the Heart is glorious, immense, boundless and timeless, far beyond the concept of "Intelligence." The activity and practice of prayer, devotion, and adoration is the way of the Heart-Soul, the fundamental "vertical" attunement with Heaven and Earth.

There are three possible distractions or distortions: cravings and compulsions in the body; obsessions and fixations in the mind; and overwhelming emotionality in the heart. But a strong, healthy and vibrant "vertical" attunement can resist, neutralize and transmute all manner of "horizontal" influences. Thus, it is divinely possible to be truly in touch with what is Really going on, within and without, Above and Below, in Heaven and Earth!

AMAZING THOUGHTS

"A new state of Consciousness gradually flows into and trans-forms everything (I) do, and so becomes integrated into (my) life." – *Eckhart Tolle*

Emotions fluctuate; feelings rise and fall like ocean swells, but there is a stillness within, a kind of "space consciousness" witnessing this daily flow. And this awareness illuminates the connection between the kind and quality of my thoughts and how they stimulate particular emotions. So I deliberately cultivate higher, wider, inspired and inspiring thoughts, ever-reminding myself of the immensity of Beauty, Truth, and Goodness!

I allow my mind to play with, to consider and entertain the highest, most sublime and divine thoughts ever thought by humans. Magnificent, glorious thoughts articulated by Great Poets, Prophets, Philosophers, Saints, and Singers of the Living Word, the ever-creating *Logos*!

Luminous Thoughts reverberating in Harmony with Flaming Archetypes and Celestial Intelligences. Thoughts alive and radiant with Kosmic Consciousness, Divine Order, Boundless Love, Infinite Compassion… Thoughts of wholeness and Perfection; of Sacred Well Being and "Eternal Delight;" of Miraculous Possibilities right *here* and *now*!

SPONTANEOUS TRANS-MUTATION/ RENEWAL

A ll along the stages of life our "bodies," vital emotional, mental, and spiritual, interact and influence one another in amazing ways. Feelings and thoughts have indeed an impact of the physical organism, for good or ill. All manner of dis-eases and dis-orders are precipitated by negative emotions and dark thoughts. For instance, grief can contribute to premature aging, and anger and anxiety to psychosomatic conditions. But the great, good news is that the miraculous healings and amazing remissions and reversions of conditions have been shown to happen under the influence of positive, uplifting states of mind. For example, the counterpart of the "premature aging" phenomenon, is what can be called "late youthing" or "golden rejuvenation." This can, and does, happen to people in their sixties or seventies, when, through a mental/ emotional "conversion" or metanoia, they allow a fresh influx of cosmic/vital energies to circulate in their "bodies," cleanse them, harmonize them and suffuse them with revitalizing Chi, Ki or Prana.

This blessed influx of "fresh Life from the Infinite" can be greatly facilitated by faith, soul-attitude, and/or all kinds of spiritual practices. Innumerable manifestations indicate that we are already surrounded and suffused by subtle, refined and sublime

Cosmic/Celestial energies that naturally and super-naturally respond to our states of soul or consciousness. We are indeed already immersed in a miraculous sea of forces and emanations, and a simple psychic shift can precipitate tremendous regeneration, trans-formation and transfiguration! Space is saturated with Grace. Relaxing and surrendering into this inherent glory can result in a spontaneous trans-mutation of our story!

"While our life is maintained by a continual inflow from the World-Soul, that inflow may vary in abundance or energy in correspondence with variations in the attitude of our own minds. Thus, faith can in actual fact draw fresh Life from the Infinite"

Frederic Myers

CEASELESS LEARNING

The universe is an infinite school where innumerable beings are ceaselessly learning. All kinds of learning, at many different levels, keep evolution unfolding. Experience, adaptation, survival, creativity, inner and outer transformations are all aspects of this continuous, cosmic Learning. Tremendous training going on, for each and all! All sentient beings are in a perpetual, unceasing state of learning. Some more or less conscious than others. Metals, plants, animals, humans (alive and dead), angels, archangels, gods and goddesses, all across the full-spectrum of terrestrial and celestial beings, are engaged in learning, both through struggle and suffering, and through play and delight.

The more consciousness, purpose and enthusiasm involved, the more joy, fun, and Light! As we prepare, coordinate, organize and set particular learning situations for our children and youth, so does Cosmic Intelligence, most lovingly, stages and choreographs wonderful evolutionary learning conditions for the best possible blossoming of souls! Through innumerable worlds, existences and bodies we are all ever-learning to blossom afresh! We are divinities in perpetual training!

A VISION

" All over the planet, across all continents and countries, in cities, towns, villages and most remote places, something wondrous is happening. Babies, children, youth and most diverse men and women are increasingly glowing with Celestial Beauty. The effulgent Radiance of this Beauty is indeed super-natural, it shines through all manner of bodies. It is the splendor of each, unique Stellar Soul, at one with the Oversoul. It is the sacred Beauty that glows in the countenance of Avatars, Mahatmas, Initiates and Saints. It is as if human organisms are becoming increasingly translucent and transparent to the Power and the Presence of the Spirit. And as more and more souls on Earth glow and shine with the Divine; with their quintessential Celestial Beauty, a tremendous trans-formation of planetary Consciousness is underway. This is because the Radiance of this other worldly Beauty is a Holy Rainbow including Peace, Harmony, Goodness, Truth, Love, Silence, Goodwill and wellbeing. And its miraculous Power instantly neutralizes and dispels ugliness, darkness, heaviness, and 'gravity.' Through eyes, bodies, minds, hearts and souls shines the Light of the World!"

LIGHT ON THE CHAKRAS

When Celestial Love descends and illuminates all centers and "chakras" (see Glossary), it brings them true freedom – the liberation of their sacred potentials and gifts.

1. As all ancestral and archetypal fears and terrors are transformed or dissolved, a new, fresh Faith becomes our true base and foundation. A total trust in the goodness, intelligence and Perfection of all there is.
2. And as Eros' eyes are opened to the glory of Life and Diversity, the drive to mate and procreate becomes the Delight of Creativity, the enthusiasm of doing and being pro-Creation and for Evolution.
3. Coming to our own center of empowerment we naturally realize the Power of Self-Reliance, ever affirming our uniqueness and asserting our magnificence.
4. The Heart opens up like a sunflower, free from the grit and grief of many yesterdays, and receptive to Heaven's Luminous Love. It expands with Infinite Joy and Compassion for all beings, and it releases the tremendous Wisdom of Divine Love, as Heart, Soul and Oversoul resonate in Perfect Harmony.
5. The throat vibrates again with The Living Logos as we recover our own Voice, the creative power of the Word

in us. So do we speak, sing and express our stellar self in Beauty, Truth and Goodness.

6. And the head, like a multifaceted and translucent crystal allows the streaming of Celestial Light or Cosmic Consciousness. Thought, intellect and reason no longer interfere with their "noise," but become multicolored precious stones reflecting the wonders of Heaven and Earth. True Intelligence shines through!

The very Heights and Depths of our whole Being, body, soul and spirit, become instantly illuminated, harmonized and integrated with the Music of Creation when suffused by Divine Love.

In essence, we *are* already this Love. It is the fundamental nature of our beingness as offspring of the unfathomable Heavens. It is not something distant, remote, inaccessible, but our very soul and substance, our "Supreme Identity." Tended by Celestial Love we are gently re-minded of the nature and purpose of our Existence: To embody, express, demonstrative and manifest the Kingdom, the Power and the Glory, in a most unique and precious way. Let the "Hidden Splendor" reveal it-self!

TRANSCENDING A TRIPLE-BLIND ECONOMY

T he original meaning of the word "Economy" points to the wise measurement and utilization of our Home-planet resources. Today, both macro and micro Economy suffer from a *triple-blindness*:

1. The exploitation, despoliation, destruction and contamination of all natural resources: mineral, plant, animal and human, and all far reaching effects on the climate, the oceans, the soils and genetic pools. This is Environmental or Eco-Blindness.

2. How the above depredation of nature has tremendous repercussions on Social Justice. The great disparity between the rich and the poor, both nations and peoples; between millionaires, billionaires and miserables across the Earth; between overweight populations and starving men, women and children between opulence and oppression, between "comfort" and despair. This is the second blindness to inequality and widespread suffering.

3. There is also a blindness regarding the nature of the universe, the existence and availability of cosmic Energies and resources, both external and internal. We are moment to moment flooded with an exuberant cornucopia of

cosmic resources, both "material" or physical, and spiritual or metaphysical, but we seem to be stuck on Fossil and Nuclear (both ancient and terrestrial), there *are* new-clear celestial forces that we remain blind to. Solar Energy is an exception, but still we have a very limited understanding of it. Several mystic-scientists such as Fechner, Steiner, Tesla, Reich, Burbank, and many others were sensitive enough to feel the presence of these universal energies.

There seems to be a fascinating correlation between the kind of energies discovered and utilized by Humankind, and how "reality" is interpreted. For instance, under the influence of nuclear power, the whole universe is explained in terms of explosions! Also, the tremendous release of fossil fuels and fossil "fumes" in the last couple of centuries seems to have contaminated not only the biosphere and the atmosphere, but also the noosphere or consciousness sphere. This has been referred to as "fossil thinking" or "dinosaur consciousness," and it is the drive behind rampant consumerism; the voracious devouring of resources; and all manner of "predatory" finances.

The philosopher John Bennett, among others, used this metaphor comparing governments, giant corporations and other influential global organizations with dinosaurs roaming, devouring and destroying the planet. But the life-cycle of these "cold blooded" rapists of the Earth is certainly coming to an end, as a profound "consciousness climate change" shall drive them to extinction and allow the thriving of truly "warm-blooded" beings, that is, beings who actually care for one-another.

The dragon of an all-consuming materialism is being subdued and transmuted by the Heavenly Knights under the wings of the Archangels; under the mantle of the Celestial Mother! These are the "Sacred Activists," that according to Andrew Harvey are both "vertically" attuned to kosmic/divine heights and depths, and "horizontally" active and creative in the deconstruction and trans-formation of all manner of Systems; social, political, religious, military and economic.

As more and more individuals, groups and organizations re-establish their balance between the natural and the super-natural worlds, there is hope for this planet in distress!

A word on "Investment". Do you know what you are supporting with your money? Unknowingly you may be supporting all kinds of "deadly" (for people & planet) industries, such as the weapons, nuclear, fossil fuels & other harmful endeavors. Every time you buy something you are supporting that industry. Also, your money in the Bank, your portfolio and your tax money go to dubious industries. What can you do? Consume less, divest, boycott and become more aware of who is doing what!

Here are some of the deadly industries to be aware of:

1. Guns & Weapons Industries.
2. Nuclear Industries, both for power and for bombs.
3. Extraction Industries. Oil ,coal, gas & mining.
4. Chemical Industries.
5. Liquor and Tobacco Industries,& many others.

NEVER ALONE, ALWAYS ALL ONE

E very single day, moment to moment, and all over the Earth, millions upon millions of souls are engaged in some kind of spiritual practice. Call it prayer, meditation, contemplation, ceremony, or ritual; it is all a sacred gesture of attunement with Heaven, with the Invisible World, with the Divine Cosmos.

This is going on all the time, unceasingly and also increasingly. Not just because there are more people on the planet, but because there is a collective, planetary awakening of Humanity to the spiritual universe. We may tend to think that the only reason why so many souls are engaged spiritually is because of their personal or family needs or difficulties. This is one of the reasons, but there are very many people, actually millions, whose inner, spiritual work and practices are for World Healing, Peace, Sanity and Light.

The Realization that all the complex world problems cannot be taken care of "horizontally" (or at the same level that they were caused, as Einstein suggested), but that radical changes, trans-formations, and unfoldments *can* happen through a collective "vertical" attunement, is incrementally and exponentially dawning upon Humanity.

Wherever we are, as soon as we engage in any kind of spiritual practice, we are never alone. Trillions of souls and angels, in this and many other worlds, are harmonizing in the immense symphony of Creation/Evolution. Reversing the well-known statement, we could say: "Practice locally, act globally." Yes, because the private, intimate, personal spiritual practices of individuals, groups, congregations, and communities have a direct effect on the whole Planet, on the whole Field of consciousness, on the whole Noosphere.

The continuous prayers, contemplations, rituals, and meditations going on in Monasteries, Ashrams, Convents, Temples, Churches, Synagogues, Pagodas, Mosques, Sanctuaries, Holy places of Pilgrimage and sacred sites around the planet, creates a tremendous "magnetic field" of "vertical attunement" that allows the circulation of Celestial Healing and Harmonizing currents.

Each open, awake and sensitive Heart-Soul is a "precipitation point" through whom Heaven and Earth can meet and blend in Luminous Love. Each Mystic, Mahatma, Saint, Paramahansa, Great Initiate, Avatar, even fledgling Disciples, is a channel, a conduit, an opening space of blooming Silence that allows torrents of benedictions upon this planet, but also any human being in harmonic resonance with the universal spirit. So, in our most secret and sacred practices we are never alone, but always all One in the Infinite!

LIVING IN THE NEW CONSCIOUSNESS

W hat is this New Consciousness? First of all it is a higher, vaster and greater dimension of consciousness. It is called *new* because it is no longer under the influence and inertia of the old intellectual, materialistic, and reductionist worldview, and specially, because it is a consciousness that is open to the ever-new freshness of timelessness, the Infinite Moment that-is.

This ever-new, unrestricted, cosmic consciousness is (metaphorically speaking) "vertical," that is, in perfect, dynamic alignment or attunement with Heaven and Earth; with all the harmonic correspondences between Above and Below; with the whole Hierarchy of Being. It is a vibrant, living and luminous Awareness that we *are* Life, cosmic Life, universal Life, the very Life pulsating and manifesting exquisitely and exuberantly across a zillion universes and worlds – Eternal Life!

It is also the Realization that we truly *are* the "Light of the World," the Creative Logos, Infinite Consciousness. And simultaneously, the existential Experience that as stellar selves we are precious, unique Individualizations of Celestial *Love*; that Divine Love is the Holy Flame in our Heart of hearts, the sacred core of our Beingness!

In the very upright, vertical Presence of this "Living Flame of Love," the "horizontal" dimension of pushing and pulling forces and influences is super-naturally neutralized and nullified.

"Time," "space," "causation," and all manner of past conditionings and interferences ("noise") dissolve as the abstractions they are. The piercing rays of a new sun burn away the mists of the old and obsolete. The superconscious, transcendental and supramental aspects of this New Consciousness, strangely enough, are simultaneously totally new, fresh and unprecedented, yet most intimately familiar and re-cognizable. A fresh awakening that is also a re-membering; a profound recalling of a state deeply known before. Plato used the word "an-amnesis," the very opposite of "forgetfulness" or oblivion; the remembrance of our true identity beyond embodiment.

In spite of the media and "state of the world" reports, the very Consciousness in the "air" today, the Noosphere, is significantly different than a hundred years ago, even thirty or forty years ago. The quantity and quality of souls attuned is increasing exponentially. Celestial "broadcasts" are being syntonized and "downloaded" rapidly by literally millions of awakening human beings, day by day. A tremendous and momentous trans-formation of planetary consciousness is certainly underway!

"We are on the cutting edge of a New Consciousness, awakening
for the whole planet. This is a time of Awakening! Know that it is
possible to move from the old to the New, easily and peacefully."

Louise Hay

WE ARE EXTRA-ORDINARY!

As innumerable saints, sages, Initiates, Mahatmas, White Magicians, Shamans and Lamas have demonstrated, and continue to demonstrate, we *do* have access to extraordinary, metanormal and miraculous forces and beings. The very "Immense Intelligence" that created us, and that is ever-creating us, has already equipped our "bodies" (vital, astral, mental, causal, buddhic and atmic) with all the functions and faculties needed to syntonize or harmonize with the Higher, subtle and Invisible worlds and their Beings. All manner of rituals, prayers, meditations, ceremonies, exercises, "yogas," adorations, sacrifices and invocations, have precisely this purpose: attunement, alignment, communication and exchange with other worlds, dimensions, realities and their inhabitants.

Through our socio-cultural conditioning we tend to be indoctrinated, programmed, "brainwashed" and even hypnotized into what is supposed to be "possible" and what is considered "impossible." These conditioned attitudes of thought and feelings drastically reduce the range of our experiences. If we happen to experience something outside of our programmed frames of reference, there is the tendency to quickly consider it as an anomaly, abnormality, weird, or even a pathological manifestation. For instance, anyone who claims to be in contact with Angels, the dead, nature spirits, gods or goddesses, avatars, saints or Mahatmas, would be easily considered to be "out of their minds," crazy or totally deluded. But the "fact" is that we already exist in a profoundly mysterious and miraculous Universe! There is no "explaining away" the miracles we call Life, consciousness, Light and Love. How does healing happen? How can consciousness exist independently of brains? How many kinds of "Light" are there? Is Love an actual Power permeating the whole universe? Is there anything that is not a miracle?

What does it mean to be gifted? We notice that there are many children and people who seem to have a special talent for this or that (art, math, music, etc), and if they demonstrate brilliancy in their gift we call them "geniuses." But the potential for genius, excellence, and true "Intelligence" exists in every-one (including in those labeled as "retarded"). There are many kinds of "Intelligences" (at least 12), and in various degrees and combinations. There are indeed tremendous potentials and possibilities latent or dormant in each human being; in each precious celestial soul embodied on this planet for a unique purpose or manifestation. The extraordinary, meta-normal, super-natural and miraculous capacities inherent (or "implicate") in our very nature are indeed "noumenal," sacred, and as they blossom, *phenomenal!*

> *"When you are inspired, your mind transcends*
> *limitations, your consciousness expands, and you*
> *find yourself in a new and wonderful world.*
> *Dormant forces, faculties and talents become alive!*
> *And you discover yourself to be greater than you ever dreamed to be."*

Attributed to Patanjali

WHALES

The passage of the whales!
From the Mendocino Headlands
I watch the vast, calm ocean.
Here and there a spout appears,
the warm, steamy breath of a
creature with a huge heart!
Very close to the coast
they gently move south.
Can they feel that they are being seen?
We are all migrating
and transmigrating through
the One, infinite Consciousness!
Who is watching our passage?
"To Be is to be perceived" said Berkeley
So we all exist, thrive, move and grow
in the light of a loving universe
contemplating our soul's journey.

AFTERWORD

I t is my delight and hope that the glimpses and insights articulated in these writings shall draw the soul curtains blocking a new sun-rise, now underway. What I have shared so far is not something never heard before, but a fresh expression of what mystics and sages across the ages have Realized and revealed through all manner of arts, sciences, discoveries and inventions (inner & outer). This is an actual re-minder of what each and all already know in the depths of their souls; the "Ground Luminosity" of Mother-Universe! The glorious Goodness of IT All!

Here I will summarize twelve key insights that constitute the essence of all meditations and contemplations included in this book.

1. There is tremendously more going on in the universe; in Heaven and Earth; in all the worlds, than traditional religions, and official sciences proclaim. Not only the Whole is without beginning and without end, that is, infinite, but so is the Kosmic Diversity of Kingdoms, Realms and Beings.

2. As human beings we are divinely designed and equipped to experience the sacred Wholeness THAT-IS. Those whose Heart's Intelligence has re-awakened; those who

are open to mystical consciousness, are able to be truly in touch with Kosmic Reality- what is really going on!

3. Being thus in-tune, alignment and harmony with the ever-unfolding Kosmos (within&without), those in the Flow are then able to willingly and joyfully cooperate with the evolutionary Process and Purpose, and to thrive with IT!

4. The challenge is that dissonance, dis-order, and all manner of interferences and distortions continue to be generated by obsolete, anachronistic, restrictive, false and insane beliefs; by the dark clouds of "cyber-noise"; by "civilization's" delusions. But, actually Seeing it for what it is, is already transcending it.

5. Neither Earth, Humanity or each individual soul is cut-off from the Kosmic Whole. The planet, all sentient beings and each unique human being are not insulated, alienated or disconnected from Universal Reality (in spite of appearances to the contrary). We already exist and unfold in a Celestial ocean of pure Life, Light and Love. And this Grace is totally available and accessible!

6. The Power of Celestial Love; the sacred/kosmic energy of Love is absolutely real! In this Omnipresence we partake and participate with innumerable worlds, Kingdoms and Realms across the galaxies. There are countless highly evolved planets , star-systems, and Celestial Beings who are totally aware of Earth's plight, and are already compassionately helping with delight!

7. Those beings referred to in all the world's ancient and folk traditions, such as Spirits of nature, Avatars, gods, goddesses, Boddhisattvas, Ancestors, demons and divinities of all kinds, do actually exist, inhabiting all Realms and Kingdoms across the infinite. So does the whole hierarchy of angels or Celestial Intelligences. We are immersed in a stellar ocean of Beingness!

8. Knowingly or unknowingly we are always under the influence of elements, forces and beings; of all kinds of vibrations and emanations. By the way we think, feel and act we tend to strike harmonic resonances with various levels of consciousness and beings. We have the possibility of choosing the kind and quality of influence we would like to be under, the Ideals and Role Models that inspire us. The Miraculous is ever-available!

9. The whole planet, including Humankind, is now undergoing a significant evolutionary stage, a critical and trans-formational cycle. But it is all happening within the Kosmic Context of greater cycles or "seasons". The "Spirit of the Times"(Zeitgeist) is not an abstract concept but an actual constellation of Higher Beings influencing and irradiating the Noosphere-Planetary Consciousness.

10. Consciousness is not a "product" or "secretion" of the brain. It exists in-dependently of bodies and permeates the whole of Nature and the Universe. It embodies itself in an infinite diversity of beings belonging to the whole spectrum of Kingdoms. Consciousness has many levels and "colors", from sub-conscious ("infrared") to super-conscious ("ultraviolet"). The whole body, not just the brain, transmits consciousness.

11. As the influx of the Kosmic NEW is accelerating, many systems, institutions, worldviews, beliefs, models and paradigms are rapidly becoming obsolete, irrelevant, outdated and out of touch with universal Reality. The inertia and momentum of the past is still strong, but weakening day by day under the Radiance of the ever-New melting the crystallizations of history. Old "maps" no longer represent the changing and shifting "territory"!

12. Every single day, now, more and more souls are re-awakening to the awe, the wonder, the grace and the glory of this boundless universe of Love. An exponential

Realization and Illumination of Hearts is happening daily all over this blessed planet. Our compassionate Kosmos is kindly and most lovingly reminding us that the Sun is up; that it's time to rise, draw the curtains, open the windows, and rejoice in the freshness of a NEW morning!

Long enough have you dream'd contemptible dreams,
Now I wash the gum from your eyes,
You must habit yourself to the dazzle of the Light,
And of every moment of your life!
Walt Whitman

APPENDIX I

WHAT IS THE NOOSPHERE?
(pronounced noh-os-sphere)

The theory of the Noosphere, is a very helpful concept to understand what is now happening on Earth. To my knowledge, the word "Noosphere" was first used by Vladimir Vernadsky, a Russian scientist; Teilhard de Chardin, a Jesuit paleontologist, and by Edouard Le Roy, a French philosopher, around 1927. Basically, noosphere derives from the Greek "Noetic" mind, knowledge or consciousness, and it refers to the human mind sphere. A mental sheath enveloping planet Earth. This mind sphere emerges from the biosphere, and it is a link with the higher, kosmic spheres of consciousness. Other thinkers who took up this concept and elaborated it further are Oliver Reiser, Aurobindo, Carl Jung, Dane Rudhyar, Rupert Sheldrake, Peter Russell, and Jose Arguelles. Though they introduced different terms such as psy-fields, collective unconscious, synchronicity, planetization of consciousness, morphogenetic fields, global brain, overmind, etc, they all describe aspects of the noosphere as a sheath of planetary consciousness.

As kosmic evolution unfolds the biosphere, so it becomes increasingly conscious of itself through the noosphere, that is human self-consciousness. In the process the technosphere (culture/civilization), and lately the cybersphere also grows and fully envelops the planet. But the actual noosphere extends far beyond all manner of technology, as it includes non-material and supra-mental domains of consciousness. Like the various levels of the atmosphere separating the planet's surface from outer space, the noosphere too, has several layers.

At the deeper level is what Jung called the "collective unconscious", a realm of ancestral and archetypal memory that connects Humankind with the Roots of Creation. History, culture, & civilization, with all the human knowledge and experience involved, is the link between the collective unconscious and the prevalent, worldwide consciousness of today's world, including all communication networks, the media, public opinion, etc. This is contemporary average, global consciousness, including the "Cybersphere". But above & beyond there are other domains or dimensions of consciousness that belong to the "Upper Noosphere". These have received various names such as; Cosmic Consciousness (R.M Bucke); Supermind (Aurobindo); Space Consciousness (E.Tolle); Oversoul; (Emerson); Etheric Christ (R. Steiner); Universal Brotherhood (Aivanhov); Hierarchy (A. Bailey), and many other labels such as the Collective Superconscious. The point here is that the Noosphere extends far into celestial realms of consciousness, and all planets with highly developed Noosphere's are in instantaneous telepathic communication (i.e.: synchronicity). Thus, we are not evolving in isolation, but partaking of this flowering across galaxies, worlds, dimensions, realms & kingdoms. Heaven is indeed, directly accessible through the re-awakened "Hearts Intelligence". The Highest imaginable is already omnipresent, fully, and most lovingly at hand!

APPENDIX II

THE IMPORTANCE OF SPIRITUAL PRACTICE

In many of the essays, especially in "Homework", I emphasize how essential it is to have a regular practice, such as prayer, meditation, contemplation, sacred rituals, inner work on one-self, or other trans-formative practices. Here I will share some suggestions.

First of all, these kinds of practices are already part of human nature; they are spontaneous, natural tendencies that express themselves in all manner of attitudes, gestures and rituals across the planet. Because we have been kosmically designed, and divinely equipped, deeply within us we have an innate wisdom guiding us regarding how to tune-in, align with other dimensions and communicate with a diversity of kingdoms and realms.

As I mentioned before: "The heart knows how to pray". There is within the soul a natural and super-natural drive towards adoration, devotion, veneration and worship. Not only in relation to higher beings, but also towards other humans, animals, plants, crystals, rivers, mountains, lakes, the sun, etc. The sacred/divine permeates the whole of nature, heaven and earth, the whole kosmos, so it can manifest through any being, creature or aspect of creation. Closely related to prayer is the soul-attitude of invocation and invitation, calling spiritual beings, Angels, Saints, Ancestors, gods or goddesses to come and share their Light, Love and Energy with us. There are millions of prayers available but the best is to make up your own, as it carries a spontaneous, creative freshness.

There is also a kind of prayer called Affirmative Prayer and it consists in using language to make statements (normally in first-person and present tense) declaring a desired condition or situation as already real. At times affirmations announce a condition that seems to contradict an actual situation, as for instance affirming, "My health is Perfect" when feeling sick at the same time. The rational here is that the affirmation or declaration is pointing to the Truth of the Big Picture, the Whole and not to temporary appearances. The practice of written and spoken affirmation can be a very good tool. Again, it is best to improvise and create your own..

Meditation across the globe is associated with stillness, silence, serenity and fine- attunement with Heaven and Earth. Sitting quietly upright, aware of your breathing, attentive of sensations, and bringing Imagination in line with creative visualizations is a common practice. Becoming conscious of all of the psychological and physiological 'noise' constantly interfering with our state of consciousness, is a first step towards serenity and silence. Body sensations or conditions, emotional states and the kind of thoughts streaming through the mind could be ongoing disruptions if not stilled and calmed in the light of conscious awareness (mindfulness).

Practically all spiritual traditions emphasize the importance of silence, quietness, solitude, stillness, rest and retreat. This is why meditation tends to be associated with relaxation, tranquility, and the overall reduction of tensions and stresses. Here I will share three basic meditations taken from timeless traditions. All three utilize an upright posture (sitting or standing) breathing, imagination and could also include arm movements.

The first one, 'Cleansing Meditation' consists in visualizing Light down pouring from above, like a radiant shower of Higher

Energy penetrating the whole body. At the same time, breathing-in this Luminous rain and absorbing the very Best imaginable: Peace, Love, Strength, Well Being, Light, Joy.... Then, when breathing-out letting the old, obsolete, negative accumulations and all that is no longer relevant, out. Here is the cleansing and purifying aspect. All accumulated negativity, tension, trauma and 'gravity' is dissolved, released and eliminated. The Ever New and positive flows in, and the old and negative leaves. The arms can be lifted in an attitude of Reception and Welcoming when breathing-in. And when expiring, the arms can be lowered towards the Earth letting go of all heaviness, density and darkness.

The second is traditionally known as the 'Metta Meditation'. The first part is the same as the above mentioned Cleansing Meditation except that all the good and the very Best is gathered and concentrated in the Heart. And from this Radiant Soul-Core it is projected far and wide as blessing for all sentient beings. This inner Sacred Sun shines in all directions as healing and uplifting benedictions for all souls in all worlds. Here too, the hands can be brought together at the chest level, and then spread out in a gesture of distributing blessings in all directions.

The third one comes from the Tibetan tradition and is known as 'Tong-Ling'. It also utilizes imagination and breathing but in a reverse way. Breathing-in, all the pain, suffering and darkness of souls is taken into the Heart's Radiant sacred core, where it is transmuted into a Healing Nectar. From that Radiant center and with the out-breath, rays of Peace, Healing and Well Being shine out to bless, uplift and illuminate all beings. So, breathing-out is the same as 'Metta'.

In summary, these three types of meditating can be described as 1- Positive in, negative out. 2- Positive in, positive out. 3- Negative in, positive out. Apart from breathing and imagination, arm and hands gestures can also be used. 1-Lifting up to receive, bringing down to release. 2- Lifting up to gather and bring hands to the heart then expanding from there. 3- Extending and gathering towards the Heart, then spreading and extending in all directions.

Of course, there are very many other kinds of meditations, such as sacred dances, martial arts, chanting, walking, kneeling, ritual prostrations, all types of yogas, sweat-lodges, sacramental ceremonies, darshan (being in the Presence of an spiritually evolved being), pilgrimages, retreats, the practice of arts, writing, journaling, contemplation, studying sacred texts, seasonal festivals/celebrations, processions, spiritual gatherings, recovery groups, inner work, and many, many more.

What is the common ground of this diversity of Practices?

It is the highest and deepest human need to re-connect, realign, fine-tune and be in Harmony with Kosmic Reality; with Heaven and Earth; with the Sacred Wholeness of Being; with the fundamental Beauty, Truth and Goodness of the Universe! And the proof is in the pudding! From Avatars to Initiates, Saints and great Masters in all fields, a magnificent rainbow of Souls have demonstrated, and continue to demonstrate, that we exist on this blessed planet, not by accident, but for a sublime, Kosmic and divine evolutionary Purpose! We are actually designed to Shine!

GLOSSARY

Ab-original: Synonymous with Primordial, Primeval, fundamental, archetypal, fully embedded in the Kosmic context of nature and the universe.

Atman: Sanskrit for Universal Soul.

"The Best of time and space": Line from a Walt Whitman poem, "I know I have the best of time and space." Synonymous with Kosmic Grace.

Bodhisattva: Sanskrit for Illumined being, human or superhuman, who willingly & compassionately returns to the darkness of "the world" in order to alleviate suffering & liberate souls.

Chakras: Sanskrit for centers or vortex of psychic energy related to particular areas of the body: 1-Base of the spine. 2-Generative organs. 3-Solar plexus. 4-Heart. 5-Throat. 6-Brow. 7-Crown

Cosmos: Greek for "order." The physical universe studied by cosmologists, astrophysicists, etc.

Dharma: Sanskit for Law,Truth,or particular destiny, individual, collective or kosmic

"Eternal Delight" From William Blake: "Energy is Eternal Delight!"

"Ever-Present Origin": Title of Jean Gebser's classic book on the unfoldment of human consciousness.

"Fresh Life from the Infinite": Expression used by Frederic Myers to describe an influx of universal life-energy.

"Great Chain of Being": Title of Arthur Lovejoy's book. It refers to the hierarchy of kingdoms in nature and beyond.

Gunas: Threefold differentiation of cosmic reality in Ancient Hindu philosophy.

"Ground Luminosity": Tibetan concept for underlying Infinite Consciousness.

Hierarchy: From the Greek: sacred order. Describes levels of beings and kingdoms both natural and supernatural. Different from man-made ranks – religions, military, etc.

Horizontal-Vertical: Common metaphor used to describe polarities such as: surface-depths; time-timelessness; tangential-radial; superficial-meaningful; compulsion-stillness; "noise"-silence; uprooted-grounded; off-centered-upright.

"Immense Intelligence": From a Ralph Waldo Emerson quote, "We lie in the lap of Immense Intelligence."

Initiate: Very highly evolved human being. Link or bridge with Higher Worlds or Kingdoms.

Interbeing: Word used by Thich Naht Hahn referring to the profound interdependence of all beings, of all Kingdoms.

Karma: Law of cause and effect, return, retribution, "boomerang effect" —"What goes around…

Kosmic: Synonymous with Holistic, Celestial, All-inclusive.

Kosmos: Greek for celestial order, infinite harmony, the Whole.

"Living Flame of Love" Expression & book title of St. John of the Cross

Logos: Greek for meaning, purpose, intelligence, law, universal reason or true knowledge. Normally mistranslated as "word."

Mahatma: Sanskrit for Great Soul or Illuminated Master.

Mahatmasphere: Realm of Higher Soul consciousness. Synonymous with "Communion of Saints," "Holy Spirit," or the "Collective Superconscious."

Mind at Large: Term used by Aldous Huxley, Joseph Campbell & others, referring to Infinite Intelligence or Kosmic Mind.

Mystic: An awakened Heart or Soul, in direct communion and communication with Heaven and Earth. A true Realist.

Noosphere: Sphere of human consciousness enveloping the planet. Its lower levels are collective consciousness as reflected in the media, "public opinion" and "trends." Its higher bandwidths reflect breakthroughs into kosmic and mystic realms of consciousness.

Paramhamsa: Sanskrit for Great Swan, or fully Realized Soul.

Saint: Spiritually awake individual, regardless of religion, whose main focus is to share Love, Light, and Service to those engulfed in darkness or distress.

Shaman: Priest, medicine man/woman, Healer, Individual initiated into the mysteries of Nature.

"Transparent to transcendence": An expression used by Karlfried Graf Durckheim to describe how both inner and outer forms can become transparent and reveal what is beyond them— the formless and absolute.

"To bear the beams of Love": from William Blake's poem: "We are put on earth, a little space, that we may learn to bear the beams of Love"

INSPIRING SOULS, SOURCES, AND RESOURCES

"We are the beneficiaries of innumerable sources." –
Ernest Holmes

As nowadays so much information is quickly available through the Cybersphere, the following list includes just the names of souls, sages, authors, poets and sources that had, and continue to have, a significant and inspiring influence on my life and work.

Omraam 'Mikhael' Aivanhov
Eben Alexander
Jose Arguelles
Sri Aurobindo
Shivapuri Baba
Michael B. Beckwith
John Bennett
William Blake
Richard Bucke
Lorna Byrne
Karlfried G. Durckheim
Wilson van Dusen
Ralph W. Emerson
Pope Francis

Shakti Gawain
Jean Gebser
Kalhil Gibran
Joel Goldsmith
Geshe Gyeltsen
Thich Nhat Hanh
Louise Hay
Andrew Harvey
David Hawkins
Lex Hixon
Ernest Holmes
Carl Jung
Krishnamurti
Dalai Lama
Federico Garcia Lorca
Ramana Maharshi
Miranda McPherson
Thomas Merton
Anita Moorjani
Michael Murphy
Pablo Neruda
Catherine Ponder
Sri Ramakrishna
Richard Rohr
Theodore Roszak
Torkom Saraydarian
Rupert Sheldrake
Rudolf Steiner
David Steindl-Rast
Robert Thurman
Tulku Thondup
Eckhart Tolle
Sir George Trevelyan
Ralph W. Trine

Swami Vivekananda

Alan Watts

Walt Whitman

Ken Wilber

William B. Yeats

Paramhamsa Yogananda

ACKNOWLEDGMENTS

My heartfelt appreciation and gratitude to all those who cooperated to the manifestation of this book:

1-The circle of my loved ones.

2-Golden Feather.

3-The Carmelite nuns of the Karmelitekloster in Sweden, who sent some loving prayers to this project.

4-Jenny Mullis, who typed the whole MSS, and

5-The Balboa Press team assisting me all the way to publication.

Thank you all!

ABOUT THE AUTHOR

Ricardo Horacio Stocker grew up in Argentina, where he studied Philosophy and Anthropology. At age 25 moved to Europe, travelled widely and attended Emerson College in Sussex, England. As a Waldorf teacher he worked in Northern Ireland (and later in Colorado and California).

After 7 years in Europe he and his new family moved to USA, where he continued his studies at Prescott College, Arizona, and Saybrook University in San Francisco. He worked in various fields of Public and Mental Health, as an Educator, Addiction Therapist, Mental Health Clinician, Bilingual Counselor, and with victims of crime and terrorism (in Spain).

For the last 16 years he has been a professor of Psychology and Communication at Mendocino College, California. As a poet he has written several anthologies of poems, both in English and Spanish. As an Optimystic his main sources of inspiration are Advaita Vedanta, Monastic Christianity, Zen and Tibetan Buddhism, and the great Initiates and mystical Poets, East & West, North& South.

He is also a musician, Storyteller, homesteader, and a loving father of four and grandfather of seven. He currently lives in the coastal mountains of Northern California.